W9-AHU-845

Grammar Lives

LANGUAGE LIVES Series:

	Language Moves
Grammar Lives	Language Works
	Language Lives

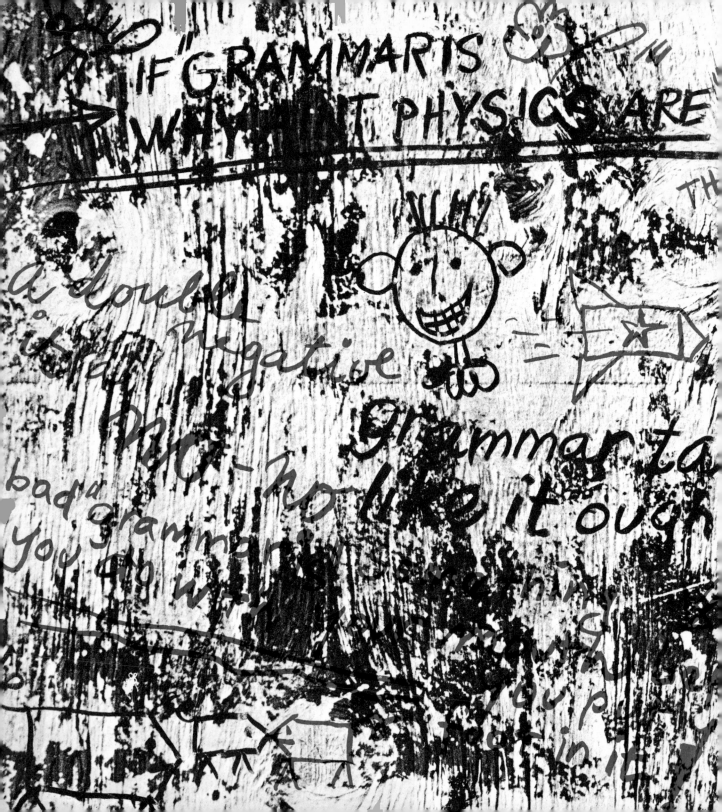

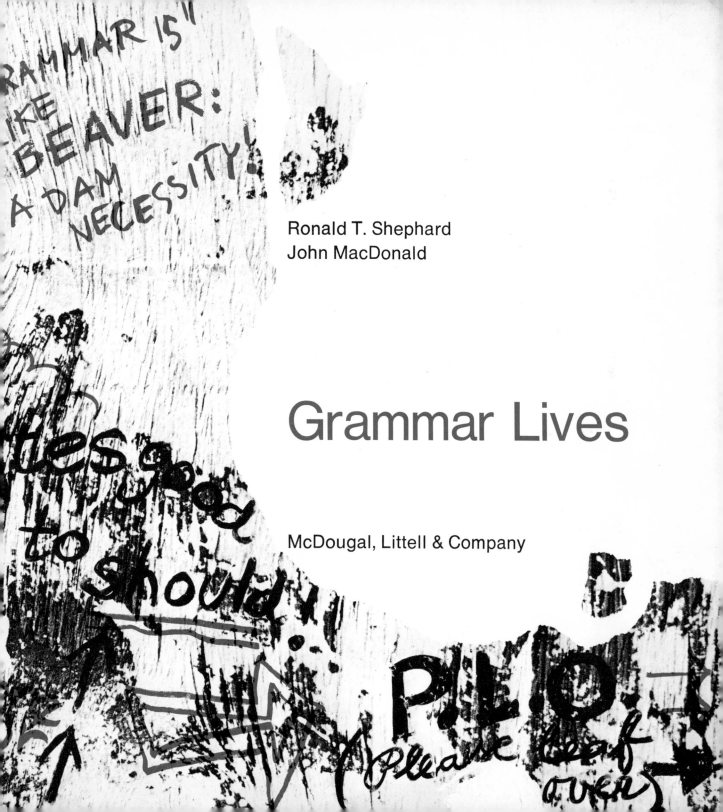

GRAMMAR IS"
IKE
BEAVER:
A DAM
NECESSITY!

Ronald T. Shephard
John MacDonald

Grammar Lives

McDougal, Littell & Company

tes good
to should!

PILO
Please leaf over

Consultant: Karen J. Kuehner
Instructional Supervisor
Department of English
Glenbrook South High School
Glenview, Illinois

Editorial Direction: Claudia Norlin

Acknowledgments: See page 184.

Illustrations: See page 185.

ISBN 0-88343-150-5

No part of this book may be reproduced or transmitted
in any form or by any means, electronic or mechanical,
including photocopying, recording, or by any information
storage and retrieval system, without permission in
writing from the Publisher.

Published 1975 by McDougal, Littell & Company,
Box 1667, Evanston, Illinois 60204. Adapted from
Grammar Is, © Thomas Nelson & Sons (Canada) Limited
1974. All rights reserved. Printed in the United States
of America.

Contents

R3.49FX

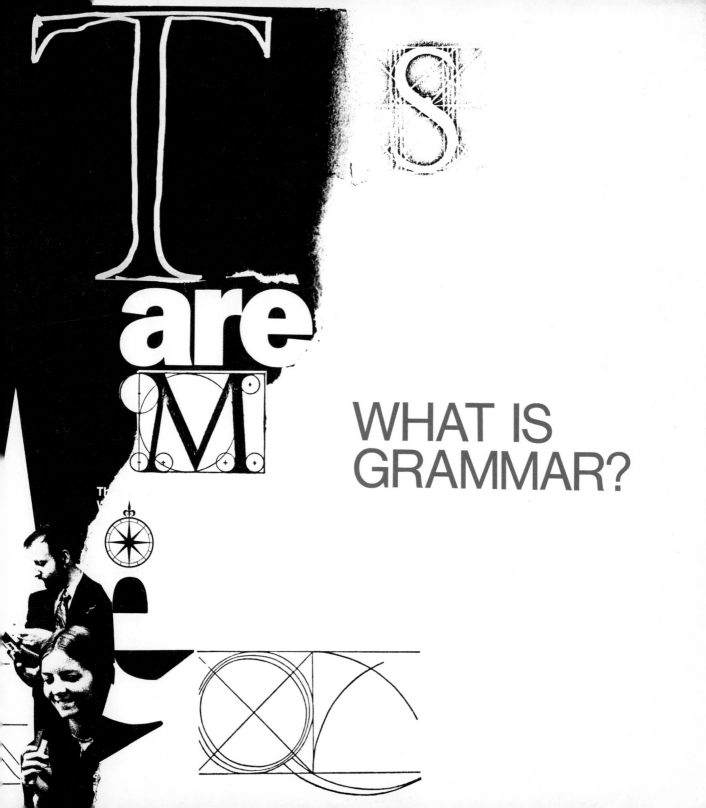

WHAT IS GRAMMAR?

INTRODUCTION

What do you think of when you hear the word "grammar"? Do you experience a specific emotional reaction? Does the prospect of beginning a study of grammar make you tingle with excitement and anticipation? Do you eagerly look forward to a satisfying experience investigating the fine points of structure in our language? If you do, then you are certainly in the minority. Most students have the same feelings for grammar that they do for a particularly foul-tasting medicine: you must take large doses of it because it is supposedly good for you, but the more you get, the more you dislike it.

Many adults have a similar reaction when they hear the word. The following paragraph, written by a high school student, summarizes the feelings of many toward grammar.

"WHY I HATE GRAMMER"

It is a hot day (to hot for school) At the front of the room, a voice drones as I sit sleeply and try to listen. Suddenly the voice swackes "Dean, sence you are so wide-awake, you may take apart the next sentence." A few laght as most have to much spring-fever to even listen. Stranulessly I decompose the sentence. At last the terrifing task is done. I relexe again. "Dean, you are intirely wrong. Now do it right" the voice growls. Wearly I try again and again and again. Oh woe! Again I'm wrong. Again I try. Oh how I wish I was dead. "Dean won't you ever learn anything. Come in after school until you learn your grammer." Fibbly I protest. But to no avail. Now you know why I can't stand grammer.

From *The Teaching of High School English,* by J. N. Hook

activities

1 Why do you think Dean dislikes grammar? Read the paragraph carefully and list his reasons.

2 Imagine that you are a member of a group which calls itself the Gift of Gab and Grammar Society, dedicated to promoting debate about the English language. Encouraged by the support of your local media, you now decide to publicize a debate on the importance of grammar.

Conveniently, it seems that within your group there are a number of points of view about grammar. Some of the members feel strongly that one can be a successful communicator without knowing anything about grammar; others are equally convinced that a knowledge of grammar increases your gift of gab.

The group's president, Ima Verb, suggests that a rally be held in the center of town, preceded by a parade. Each of you is to create a sign which states your own position. The sign must clearly give your attitude—pro or con— plus a specific reason why grammar should or should not be studied.

When the group is assembled with signs, look for those who have ideas similar to your own. (There should be at least two factions—pro-grammar and anti-grammar—and possibly some neutrals or extremists.) Choose a spokes-man for each faction who will present a two-minute speech stating the views of that group. A panel of experts (chosen beforehand by the group) should judge the winner.

GRAMMAR AND USAGE

When we discuss grammar, we should be sure we know what the word means. In a nontechnical sense, grammar is usually taken to mean "correctness in speaking and writing." As this is a common definition and one of several that can be found in a good dictionary, it deserves attention.

According to this definition, people are guilty of "bad grammar" if they use such expressions as "I ain't," "He don't," and "She done it." The modern practice, however, is to refer to such matters as usage. *Usage* refers to our choice of words in speaking and writing, our language behavior. *Grammar,* on the other hand, refers to the way we put those words together, the structure of our language. Strictly speaking, when we talk about the grammar of a language, we are not talking about the preferred choices among words and phrases, but about the system of language, the way we combine words to produce meaning.

Actually, if you are a native speaker of English, you are already an expert in English grammar. You have learned the rules and can apply them to produce or to understand an infinite variety of sentences. Practically every sentence you spon-taneously speak or write is a new event; you certainly have not memorized a list of phrases or sentences to be used in communication with others. You have a marvelous apparatus in your brain which enables you to use the rules of English grammar to produce a constant flow of new sentences. If you are skeptical and wonder whether you really know the rules, look at the following sentences:

1. He gave the Vice-President a flower for his lapel.
2. He a flower the Vice-President for his lapel gave.
3. The moon is quite bright tonight.
4. The moon are quite tonight bright.
5. The glibsters are mobling in the gabatorium.
6. All students can run a mile in two minutes.
7. My brother is a bicycle.

Any native speaker of English who understands the meanings of the words can recognize imme-diately that numbers 2 and 4 do not conform to the basic structure of English sentences. He can probably also recognize that number 5 does conform to that structure, even though it contains three nonsense words. Numbers 6 and 7 are also "grammatical" even though they are not true. If you understand the difference between gram-mar and usage, you should be able to explain why the first of the following two sentences, although not considered standard usage, is grammatical, while the second is ungram-matical.

He ain't got no money.
He any money not does have.

GRAMMATICAL MEANING

scrawny the ate chicken man plump the

The above words are all simple English words with obvious meanings. However, although you know the meaning of each word, you cannot make sense of the statement as it is written. Rearrange the words and write them so that they form a meaningful statement. Now you have a typical English sentence that conveys meaning. But everyone in the class does not have the same sentence. As you were rearranging the words you probably realized other possible arrangements. Write these down also. You should have four different sentences.

Examine the structure of the four sentences closely. The difference in them indicates an important principle of English grammar. Here you have four sentences containing exactly the same words. And yet, without any change in the form of the words themselves you are able to combine them into four separate sentences, four patterns that produce completely different meanings. Obviously there must be some factor in English, aside from the meaning of individual words, that produces total meaning. In our example, this factor determines not only what will be eaten, but also how it will probably taste. What is this factor?

4

MODERN GRAMMAR

It may seem strange to you that there are different theories about English grammar. But as our knowledge expands, we make new discoveries in many fields. Consider how much more we know today about such subjects as chemistry, physics, mathematics, and medicine than we did fifty years ago. We also know much more about our language and the way it operates.

One of the things we have learned is that English is structurally a very different language from Latin. Unfortunately, many of the so-called "rules" of grammar, first set down in the seventeenth and eighteenth centuries, are based on Latin rules. The early scholars who first wrote the English grammar books made the mistake of equating English with Latin, and of assuming that many of the rules for Latin could be applied to English. Many people today still labor under that mistaken belief.

One illustration of the many differences between Latin and English is the principle you discovered on page 4—the patterning of words in an English sentence—*word order*. In English, the relative positioning of words in a sentence is sometimes as important as the actual meaning of the words and, in fact, helps to give words their meaning. English grammar, then, depends largely on the principle of word order. The way words pattern together in English produces a meaning that adds to or clarifies the dictionary meanings of a word—a *grammatical meaning.*

Latin grammar, on the other hand, does not rely on word order. It conveys essential information about the relationship of words in a sentence by changing the form of the words themselves, which is called *inflection.*

Look, for example, at these two sentences in Latin which are translated into English:

Maria Robertum amat.   Mary likes Robert.
Mariam Robertus amat.   Robert likes Mary.

We can easily see that the meaning of these Latin sentences depends on inflection, while the meaning of the English sentences depends on word order.

She kicked him only yesterday.

WORD ORDER

The caption for the picture shown above clearly states what is happening in the picture. We can add certain shades of meaning, however, by experimenting with the placement of one word in various positions in the sentence. Try inserting the word "only" in different positions. How many different shades of meaning do you get? Notice how a simple change in word order can alter the meaning of the sentence.

Discuss in class how word order determines meaning in the following pairs of sentences:

a Clothing makes the man.
   The man makes clothing.
b George is sick.
   Is George sick?
c Bill called his girlfriend pretty.
   Bill called his pretty girlfriend.
d Running from the accident, we met Bill.
   We met Bill running from the accident.
e Yesterday I paid for the new suit I bought.
   I paid for the new suit I bought yesterday.
f Tomorrow will be a day off for me.
   Tomorrow will be an off day for me.

INFLECTION

Word order is the most important feature of modern English grammar. Inflection also has a function in our grammar, but it is not nearly as important as it is in a language like Latin. When the word *inflection* is used in this book, it refers to any changes made in the form of a base word to indicate a grammatical relationship. Most nouns inflect, for instance, to show plural by adding "s" or "es." Verbs like "walk" or "talk" inflect to show past time by adding "ed": "walked," "talked." You are probably familiar with the word "whom" which is the inflected form of "who."

Imagine that you discovered the following sentence in a book:

As native speaker of English, you constantly make use of inflectional rule although you do not use they as much as speaker of English do in the past.

You would be puzzled by some irregularities in the sentence, but you would still be able to understand it. The reason that the sentence seems awkward is that none of the normal inflections of English have been used.

Rewrite the sentence making the necessary changes in inflection. Using the changes you have made in the sentence as a guide, list three uses of inflection in modern English.

Imagine that your teacher asks your class the following question: "Who cleaned the chalkboards this morning?" Which of the following replies would be most appropriate?

a Him and me cleaned them.
b Him and I cleaned them.
c Me and he cleaned them.
d He and I cleaned them.
e I and he cleaned them.

Notice that in each sentence you may use either "I," which is the form for the doer of an action, or the inflected form "me," which is the form for the receiver of an action. Similarly, you may use "he" or the inflected form "him." There is obviously one sentence more appropriate than the others in this situation. But any native speaker of English could easily understand any of the sentences. What does that fact tell you about the relative importance of word order and inflection in English? Which one is the more vital for understanding English?

FORM CLASS WORDS
AND STRUCTURE WORDS

Divide the class into groups according to the instructions of your teacher. After you have been assigned to a group, complete the following instructions:

1 List the parts of speech in your notebook. Check with the other members of your group to see if you all have the same ones.
2 Write three examples of each part of speech. Discuss your examples with the other members in your group. If you have any example that the group is uncertain about, choose another.
3 Examine your list carefully. Try to decide which are the four most important parts of speech in English.
4 Discuss your ideas with the other members of the group, and decide together which are the four most important.
5 Present the findings of your group to the rest of the class, and come to a final class decision.

Possibly your group had difficulty trying to classify certain words. This is to be expected because there are some words that we cannot classify until we see how they are used in a sentence. You might have used the word "run" as an example of a verb, thinking of the sentence, "He runs very fast." But someone else may have given "run" as an example of a noun, thinking of the sentence, "She has a run in her stocking," or, "He goes for a long run every morning." Both of you would have been correct. We have many words in English that can function as different parts of speech.

You have discussed in your groups the four most important parts of speech: nouns, verbs, adjectives, and adverbs. Practically all of the words in the English language belong to one of these four categories. We call them *form classes*.

FORM CLASSES

Nouns, verbs, adjectives, and adverbs belong to the same class because each one occurs in a certain set of positions in English sentences. They are called form classes because many of them have special forms — endings and the like — which set them off from one another. They have special features of form that enable us to recognize them. They are the words that provide the substance of our sentences, the chief tools we use in communicating with each other. Form classes are open: new words are constantly being added as the language changes.

The form class to which a word belongs may vary according to the way the word is used. Consider the following sentences:

She marks the changes.
She changes the marks.

We can recognize immediately that "marks" is not the same kind of word in the first sentence that it is in the second. We can recognize a similar difference with "changes." But, since the form classes are clearly marked by certain signals, we have no difficulty understanding each sentence. If we were not given these signals, we could not understand the sentences.

STRUCTURE WORDS

Baby Swallows Fly

What are the two possible interpretations of the above headline? What is the cause of the uncertainty? Add a word or words to the sentence to make the meaning clear, one way or the other. Do the same with the following headlines:

Ship Sails Soon

STUDENT DEMANDS CHANGE

Plant Flowers Early

Seal Trains at Night

Swallow Drinks Quickly

Examine the words you used to clarify the headlines. The first could be clarified by adding the words ''a'' and ''the'': "The baby swallows a fly." The words ''a'' and ''the'' signal that ''baby'' and ''fly'' are nouns and that the sentence indicates an infant is swallowing an insect. But if you omitted the signal word ''a'' before ''fly,'' then your sentence would read, ''The baby swallows fly.'' In this case ''fly'' would be a verb, and the sentence would have a completely different meaning.

Words like ''a'' and ''the,'' whose main purpose is to signal the relationship of words in the sentence to each other, are called *structure words.* As the name implies, their main function is to make the structure of sentences clear. They are signaling words, more important for the relationship they indicate between form classes than for any meaning they carry. Form classes provide the substance of our sentences; structure words give order to that substance. The relationship of the two classes to each other can be compared to the main parts of a suspension bridge: towers and some form of suspension cables. Form class words are the towers which provide the basic strength of the bridge; structure words are the suspension cables which hold the bridge together.

Structure words are a closed class, with new words rarely ever being added. They cannot be identified by features of form such as word endings; usually they cannot be inflected. Prepositions, conjunctions, definite and indefinite articles, and certain pronouns are some of the key structure words in English.

Word order, inflection, and structure words are the principal grammatical devices which signal meaning. The following nonsense sentence illustrates how they operate.

Gop farlers bopized o ruction

The sentence, as it stands, makes no sense whatsoever. But if we substitute English structure words for some of the nonsense words, the sentence becomes more meaningful.

The farlers bopized *a* ruction

By the substitution of two words—"The" and "a"—we have provided a more meaningful structure for the nonsense words. "The" and "a" are structure words which are used in English primarily to signal nouns. Consequently, when we insert them into our nonsense sentence, they signal that "farlers" and "ruction" might be nouns, form class words. Make use of the other grammatical devices that signal meaning, word order, and inflection, to prove that "farlers" and "ruction" are in fact nouns as they are used here. By applying the same clues, what information can you deduce about the word "bopized" as it is used in this sentence?

9

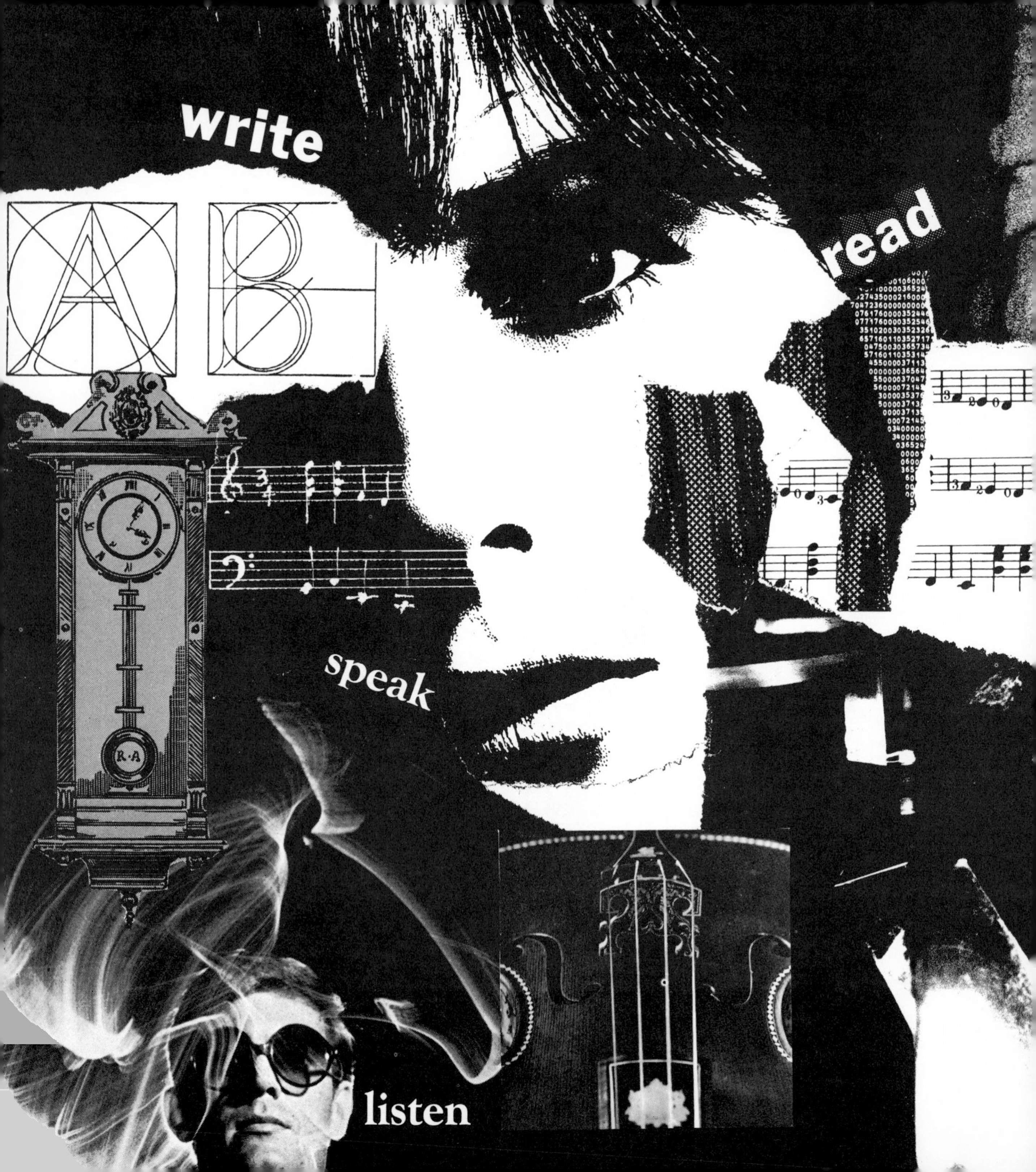
write
read
speak
listen

THE PARTS
OF SPEECH

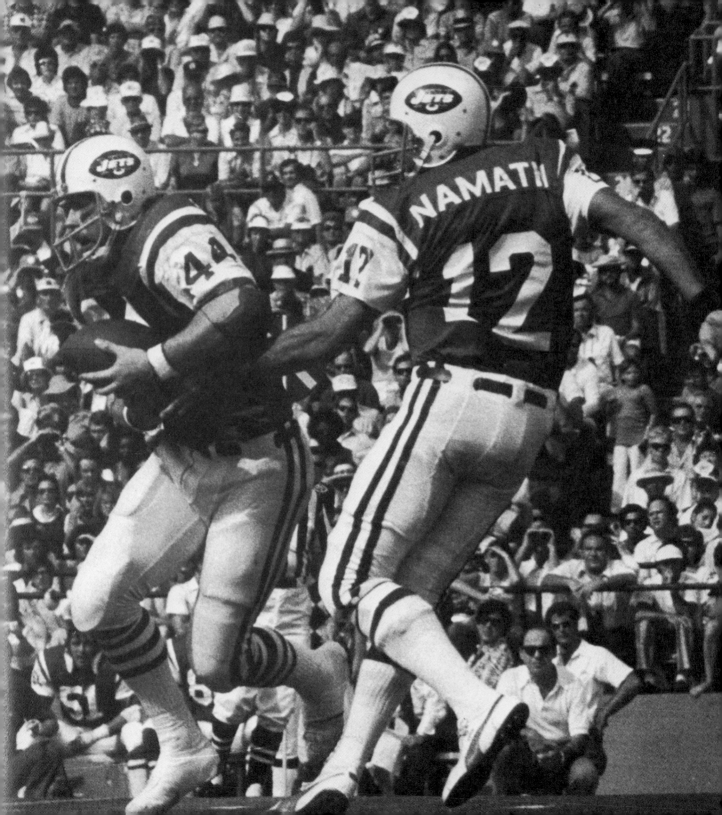

DISCOVERING NOUNS

The photograph on the opposite page was taken during an exciting moment in professional sports. Examine the picture and answer the following questions:

1 What is the name of the game these men are playing?
2 For which team do they play?
3 Can you name either of the players shown here?
4 Do you know what position either one plays?
5 What is the maneuver called that they have just completed?
6 Name some pieces of equipment shown in the picture.

These questions probably seem rather childish and obvious to you, especially if you are a football fan. But stop for a moment and look at the words you used to answer the questions—"football," "New York Jets," "Joe Namath," "quarterback," "handoff," "helmet," "face mask," "jersey," "knee pads," and so forth. What do they all have in common? Imagine how difficult it would be to communicate, to discuss a football game, for instance, if our language did not contain a supply of words like these, words which are used primarily to name things, people, and activities.

Such words are called nouns. Perhaps you have learned the traditional definition of a noun: "a word that names a person, place, or thing." While it is true that nouns are naming words, there are problems, however, with such a limiting definition. Consider the following sentence:

Joe Namath is wearing a white helmet.

Which words in the sentence are nouns? What part of speech is "white"? What is its function in the sentence? But doesn't the word "white" name a color? According to the definition, then, it should be a noun. Obviously, it isn't. Therefore the definition does not apply in this case.

Rather than worrying about how to define nouns, we should be more concerned with observing how nouns actually operate in our language and learning how to use them effectively. The grammar of our language provides us with certain signals which identify nouns: inflection, structure words, and word order.

INFLECTION TO SHOW PLURAL

Ask a kindergarten child what he sees in the picture on page 12. He will probably reply "men" or "football players." He has already learned those rules in English grammar which enable him to distinguish between singular and plural, between oneness and more than oneness. Although he probably couldn't explain the rule, it has become a part of his built-in language mechanism. He learned at an early age, by imitating older children and adults, that we normally form plurals in English by adding an "s" or a "z" sound to a word (cat—cats[s]; dog—dogs[z]). He also learned that there were other words like "church" or "bush" to which you could not add a simple "s" sound; the resulting words would be too difficult to pronounce. For words like these he had to add another sound, which we represent in our writing systems by the letter "e" (church—churches[iz]; bush—bushes[iz]).

The Media Are Not Singular

As sure as the ~~crocus crocuses~~ croci that come up in the spring, Greek and Latin words have always popped up to decorate the ~~incunabulum~~ incunabula of a writer who wanted his ~~memorandum~~ memoranda to sound more important than ~~it is~~ they are. The data ~~is~~ are not complete, but it appears that this ~~phenomena~~ phenomenon occurs most often nowadays within the ~~strata~~ stratum of people concerned with newspapers, magazines, television and radio—in a word, media. Trouble is, the media ~~is~~ are not singular; ~~it is~~ they are plural, as ~~is~~ are candelabra. According to this ~~criteria~~ criterion, the first thing on the ~~agendum~~ agenda should be to call a halt to all of ~~this~~ these errata.

From *Time,* June 6, 1970

activities

1 a Imagine that you are programming a computer to translate other languages into English. You must provide it with a set of general "rules" for the formation of the plural. Begin with the basic rule that English nouns form their plural by adding "s." By examining the following list of plurals, construct three other rules for the computer.

churches	valleys
turkeys	waltzes
allies	ladies
gases	ditches
taxes	campuses
memories	juries
monkeys	flashes
bushes	waxes

b From the following examples construct a rule which will guide the computer in forming the plural of nouns ending in "o" preceded by a vowel.

rodeo—rodeos	studio—studios
cameo—cameos	radio—radios
igloo—igloos	taboo—taboos

c Unfortunately, there are classes of nouns in English which do not form their plurals according to any regular "rules." The computer will have to store the following examples in its memory bank:

Nouns ending in "o" preceded by a consonant: some add "s," others "es," and still others "s" or "es."

"s"	"es"
pianos	heroes
sopranos	tomatoes
dynamos	echoes

"s" or "es"
mosquitos or mosquitoes
zeros or zeroes
cargos or cargoes

Nouns ending in "f" or "fe": some change the "f" to "v" before adding the plural ending, others do not, others have more than one plural form.

"s"	"ves"	"s" or "ves"
beliefs	knives	scarfs or scarves
dwarfs	lives	hoofs or hooves
chiefs	leaves	calfs or calves

Some nouns do not form their plurals by adding "s" or "es."

- some add "en": children, oxen
- some keep the plural in their original language: alumni, media
- some undergo an internal change: men, mice
- some have the same form for singular or plural: deer, trout

2 Assume that our computer is still not fully programmed. You have conducted a trial run with it, and it is incapable of printing out the plurals of nouns. Instead, it simply attaches the label (PL) to the base word. Rather than printing "boys" or "men" it uses "boy" (PL) or "man" (PL). Translate the following sentences:

a Most library (PL) suffer heavy loss (PL) from thief (PL) who steal book (PL).
b For breakfast we had egg (PL), potato (PL), fish (PL), and three loaf (PL) of bread.
c Many man (PL) become hero (PL) because of major crisis (PL).
d Most employer (PL) offer no apology (PL) for the criterion (PL) they use in selecting their vice-president (PL).

3 Our computer is confused. It has asked the following questions. Try to make up five similar ones.

If the plural of "mouse" is "mice," why isn't "spice" the plural of "spouse"?

If the plural of "index" is "indices," why isn't "Kleenices" the plural of "Kleenex"?

If the plural of "thief" is "thieves," why isn't "chieves" the plural of "chief"?

4 You have been hired for the summer by a publisher. A writer whose manuscript you are editing has asked you to check the plurals of the following words, all of which are unusual forms. Write the plurals.

analysis, datum, Negro, wolf, board of education, brother-in-law, sheep, phenomenon, cupful, formula

5 Examine the following sentences uttered by young children. Discuss how these sentences shed light on the manner in which young children learn the "rules" for forming the plural of nouns.

"Daddy, there are two mans at the door."
"We have ten childrens in our class."
"Mommy, can I sit on your laps?"
"My foots are cold!"

INFLECTION TO SHOW POSSESSION

Another characteristic feature of nouns is that they inflect to form possessives by adding an apostrophe and "s" or an apostrophe alone. By examining the following phrases, discover the rules for forming possessives:

a boy's book, the children's party, several girls' dresses, Mr. Jones' car, the men's coats, a lady's hair, many ladies' hair, the duchess' hat

You should have a rule for each of the following:

- the possessives of singular nouns
- the possessives of singular nouns ending in "s"
- the possessives of plural nouns
- the possessives of plural nouns ending with "s"

DERIVATIONAL SUFFIXES

We have seen how nouns add suffixes (endings) to form the plural and the possessive. These changes in form are called *inflectional suffixes* Inflectional suffixes are not the only suffixes which distinguish nouns, however. Consider the following list of nouns. What are some of the characteristic noun endings?

kindness, speaker, departure, happiness, deduction, scientist

These suffixes are called *derivational suffixes* because words formed with them are derived from other words or parts of words.

kind + ness = kindness
speak + er = speaker
depart + ure = departure

The following statement was made by a young high school student in response to a teacher's question about the play *Julius Caesar:*

CAESAR DID NOT ACT BECAUSE HIS FEARNESS WAS OVERCOME BY HIS PROUDNESS.

The student knew the play, but he had some trouble with his nouns. What was his problem?

activities

1 Unfortunately, our computer is not yet capable of forming nouns by adding suffixes to base words. It simply prints the base word and attaches the label (DER) to indicate a derivational suffix. For instance, rather than "kindness" it prints "kind(DER)"; for "speaker" it prints "speak(DER)." In the following examples, translate the "computer noun" in the second sentence of each pair.

a We all knew he was a *loyal* man. His loyal(DER) was beyond question.
b They will *deduct* more money next month. It seems to be a necessary deduct(DER).
c I shall *pay* promptly. My prompt pay(DER) will be appreciated.
d I always try to be *prompt*. I hope my prompt(DER) is appreciated.
e I hope you do not *fail*. Your fail(DER) would be unfortunate.
f The actor is *vital*. His vital(DER) is obvious.
g He can *act* very well. He is a good act(DER).
h He can *play* very well. He is a good play(DER).
i You should not *lie* about things. People will call you a lie(DER).
j She was very *friendly* to me. Her friendly(DER) was obvious.

2 Write two nouns that use each of the following suffixes. Use each noun in a sentence.

hood, ist, dom, age, ster, ment, cy, ence, ance

DETERMINERS

On page 8 you learned something about the group of words in English called structure words, words whose main function is to indicate relationships between form class words. Noun determiners are structure words whose main function is to signal that a noun will follow.

17

The following headline contains no noun determiners.

Swallow Drinks Quickly

What are the two meanings that you could take from this headline? What is the cause of the uncertainty? Notice that a noun determiner, by signaling that one of the words is to be considered a noun, can clarify the meaning:

(A)Swallow Drinks Quickly

If you were to insert a noun determiner before another word, however, the meaning would change.

Swallow (The) Drinks Quickly

The noun determiners "the" and "a," the definite and indefinite article, are the most commonly used.

WORD ORDER—NOUN POSITIONS

It is impossible to classify nouns simply by their position in the sentence, because other parts of speech may be used in noun positions or "slots." But we can recognize the most common noun positions and use these along with the other signals we have been discussing: inflection and noun determiners. The nouns in the following sentences occupy the usual noun "slots" in a sentence. Study these sentences and decide on the three most common noun positions.

1 Harry Hunkoman is a wrestler.
2 Harry is usually a mild man, except in the ring.
3 At school Harry never liked grammar.
4 Many wrestlers are admired by their fans.

Test Frame for Nouns

A test frame is a sentence containing blank spaces into which words can be inserted to determine their part of speech. A common test frame for nouns is the following:

(The)_____is/are (good).

"The" is in parentheses because it does not have to be used for all nouns. You would use it for words like "book," "apple," and "boy," but not for words like "honesty" or "John Lennon." "Good" is also in parentheses because it is not necessary that you use this particular adjective. For some words that you are testing you may want to substitute "bad." Try some words suggested by your teacher or classmates in the test frame to determine whether or not they could be nouns.

activities

1 The following excerpt from Lewis Caroll's "Jabberwocky" poem (from *Through the Looking Glass*) is an example of the use of "nonsense" words that behave very much like typical English words. Pick out the nouns and explain the clues that helped you.

> 'Twas brillig and the slithy toves
>   Did gyre and gimble in the wabe;
> All mimsy were the borogoves,
>   And the mome raths outgrabe.

2 Assume that the following sentences were written by a computer which was programmed in this manner:

a For inflectional suffixes to show plural, it attached (PL) to the base word: "man (PL)" = "men."
b For inflectional suffixes to show possession, it attached (POSS) to the base word: "girl (POSS)" = "girl's."
c For noun derivational suffixes, it attached (DER) to the base word: "happy (DER)" = "happiness."

Where more than one kind of suffix was needed, the computer attached two signs to the base word in the proper order: "arrive (DER) (PL)" = "arrivals," "boy (PL) (POSS)" = "boys' " and "inspect (DER) (POSS)" = "inspectors'."

For example, the following is a computer print-out and its translation:

The doctor (POSS) need for private (DER) conflicted with his patient (PL) (POSS) friendly (DER).

The doctor's need for privacy conflicted with his patients' friendliness.

Now translate these sentences from "computer English" to English.

a Girl(PL) in our society who want free (DER) from household duty(PL) should not marry.
b Many famous science(DER)(PL) have been persecuted for their belief(PL).
c Mr. Jones(POSS) attorney(PL) advised him to beware of thief(PL).
d The foreign student(POSS) main desire was to live in a democrat(DER).
e Many young act(DER)(PL) lose friend(PL) because of jealous(DER).
f The duchess(POSS) will left all her worldly possess(DER)(PL) to her seven child (PL).
g In the play *Julius Caesar,* Brutus(POSS) reluctant(DER) to join the conspire(DER) is overcome by his love of Rome.
h Many of Shakespeare(POSS) hero(PL) are tricked by the offer of friend(DER) from a villain.
i The Jones(PL)(POSS) new dentist was very pleased that their son had no cavity(PL).
j Sometimes a boss(POSS) idea of humble(DER) does not coincide with an employ(DER)(POSS).

3 Pick out the nouns in the following nonsense sentences. Making use of all the grammatical signals that you can, justify your choice of each noun.

a A gorcher was quiffing in the zipilution.
b All the merrimacs funtimed the holidusks.
c A forler's gofdom is hibby.

USING NOUNS EFFECTIVELY

Look again at the photograph on page 12. In your initial discussion of it, you found that the words used to identify the people and things were all nouns: "football," "New York Jets," "Joe Namath," "quarterback." Even in this short list, we can see two different types of nouns: proper and common. Words such as "Joe Namath," "New York," and "National Football League," which name particular people, places, and things, are called *proper nouns*. They always begin with capitals. All other nouns are *common nouns*.

When we want to refer to a group, we use a *collective noun,* such as "team," "crowd," or "committee." A collective noun is singular in form but stands for a group of people or objects.

activity

1 A copywriter tries to design ads that will attract your attention and remain in your memory. Explain the grammatical device used to attract your attention in the "Twigs" ad on page 21.

2 Will the name of his product be remembered by readers of the ad? Explain.

3 List all the nouns in this ad. Why are there so few proper nouns?

4 In the bottom right corner, we are told that "Twigs is a collective term." Why do you think this part of the ad was included?

5 Is this a successful ad? Explain.

NABISCO

YOU'LL FIND QUALITY IN OUR CORNER.

Twigs is*here.

mild'n mellow new snack!

PRESS IN UNDER SPOT ▼ THEN LIFT TOP TO OPEN

NABISCO

ONION flavored

TWIGS

snack sticks WITH POPPY SEEDS

Twigs is tasty little breadsticks in two flavors: sesame cheese and new onion poppy.

Twigs is good company for cheese.

Twigs is wonderful for adding flavor and crunchiness to salads.

Twigs is different with dips.

Twigs is for eating with meals.

*Twigs is a collective term which means you can say "Twigs is baked by Nabisco" or "Twigs are baked by Nabisco." They is. And they are.

SPECIFIC AND GENERAL NOUNS

Look at the photograph on page 12 and, using only nouns, identify the two people pictured there. You have a variety of nouns available to you. You can be very general and refer to them as "human beings." Being a little more specific, you might refer to them as "males." Probably, however, you would refer to them as "athletes" or, more specifically, as "football players." The most specific nouns you could use would be proper nouns, the actual names of the players. The noun "Joe Namath," for instance, refers to only one particular person, a well-known quarterback in professional football.

The noun "Joe Namath" is a symbol we use to stand for the person it represents, its *referent* "Joe Namath" is a specific noun because it has only one referent. "Football player" is more general because it refers to a greater number of referents. "Athlete" is still more general because it refers to even more. "Human being" is, of course, the most general noun in this list because it has many referents—the entire population of the world.

Think of specific and general nouns as rungs in a ladder: the top is the most general word, the bottom the most specific. The rungs in between contain words in ascending order of generality.

CONCRETE AND ABSTRACT NOUNS

Group the following words into two lists so that the words in each list have something in common with each other.

honor, apple, Bill Cosby, courage, security, girl, skunk, rose, love, evil, song, happiness, perfume, truth

Explain what the words in each of your lists have in common with each other. How do they differ from the words in the other list?

If you have sorted the words into a group containing nouns with specific referents that actually exist in the physical world and a group that refer to ideas or mental concepts that do not exist by themselves in the physical world, then you have discovered the difference between *concrete nouns* and *abstract nouns.* Concrete nouns name things which can be perceived by our senses. We can taste an ''apple,'' smell a ''rose'' or a ''skunk,'' hear a ''song'' and see a ''Bill Cosby.'' Abstract nouns have less definite referents. They name a quality that an object may possess but that cannot be detached so that it has a separate existence from that object. When we hear or read the words ''courage,'' ''happiness,'' or ''evil,'' we cannot visualize a specific referent for these words. We cannot perceive these things by themselves. Rather, we have to relate them to concrete words: a ''courageous'' soldier, ''happiness is a warm puppy,'' an ''evil'' villain.

A good general rule to follow in your own writing is to be as specific and concrete as possible. Use specific nouns to ''show'' your reader

If those who have studied the art of writing are in accord on any point, it is on this: the surest way to arouse and hold the attention of the reader is by being specific, definite, and concrete. The greatest writers—Homer, Dante, Shakespeare—are effective largely because they deal in particulars and report the details that matter. Their words call up pictures.

From *The Elements of Style,* by Strunk and White

rather than ''tell'' him. A specific, concrete noun forces your reader to visualize a clear mental image. Which of the following, for instance, suggests a clearer picture to you?

We were favorably inclined towards the sartorial refinement of the diplomat in his last media appearance.

or

We were impressed with the French ambassador's elegant clothing in his interview on Channel 9 last Saturday night: gray suit and vest, white shirt, blue polka dot tie, and black shoes.

Sometimes writers who are not sure what they want to say try to disguise their lack of ideas by using general and abstract terms. Others try to impress the reader with their learning by their use of generalities and abstractions. The result, unfortunately, is vagueness and fuzziness rather than clarity and precision. George Orwell, the famous writer, satirized the tendency of some writers to smother their reader with abstractions. The following is his "translation" of a passage from the Bible:

Objective consideration of contemporary phenomena compels the conclusion that success or failure in competitive activities exhibits no tendency to be commensurate with innate capacity, but that a considerable element of the unpredictable must invariably be taken into account.

George Orwell

Compare the above version with the original:

"I returned, and saw under the sun, that the race is not to the swift, nor the battle to the strong, neither yet bread to the wise, nor yet riches to men of understanding, nor yet favour to men of skill; but time and chance happeneth to them all."
    Ecclesiastes, IX, v.11.

The specific noun, however, is not always better than the general; neither is the concrete always superior to the abstract. Without abstract words we would never be able to think about and discuss ideas and ideals common to all mankind: honor, love, happiness, beauty, faith. General nouns help us sum up and group things together. Without them communication would be much more complicated. It is certainly more convenient to post a sign saying "NO DOGS" than one saying "NO COLLIES, SPANIELS, DACHSHUNDS, TERRIERS, ST. BERNARDS, BULLDOGS . . ."

24

Without general nouns, imagine the problems owners would have identifying their stores.

activities

1 Make your own language ladders, similar to the one on page 22, for each of the following words. The words may occur anywhere on the ladders. Make sure that each ladder is at least five words long.

school
Julius Caesar
basketball
mammal
poet
Ford Pinto
quadruped

2 In the following sentence we are not given much specific information: "A vehicle hit a human being." We can make the sentence more specific by constructing a series of sentences in which the nouns become less general.

A vehicle hit a human being.
An automobile hit a girl.
A Cadillac hit Susie Smith.

Notice that in each of these sentences the more specific the nouns are, the clearer the message is. Try constructing your own sentences (at least three) for each of the pictures on pages 26 and 27. When you finish, choose one picture and write a brief story related to it, using specific, concrete nouns.

"I have a pet at home"

"Oh, what kind of a pet?"

"It is a dog."

"What kind of a dog?"

"It is a St. Bernard."

"Grown up or a puppy?"

"It is full grown."

"What color is it?"

"It is brown and white."

"Why didn't you say you had a full-grown, brown and white St. Bernard as a pet in the first place?"

"Why doesn't anybody understand me?"

3 In the illustration on this page we see a series of statements clarifying a general noun—"pet." Using the illustration as a model, try the following game in class. One person begins by making a statement containing a general noun. His statement should be similar in structure to "I have a pet at home." Other students in the class then try to identify the specific object by asking questions. When they have identified it, another student begins. Keep a record of the number of questions needed to identify each object.

4 The ad on page 29 probably doesn't make too much sense to you because some of the nouns have been left out. Each time a noun has been removed, there is a symbol indicating whether the noun was a common noun (CN), a proper noun (PN), or a plural common noun (CNP). Make up your own ad for this product, rewriting the story by inserting a noun for each symbol. The only rule is that you must insert the correct number and kind of nouns. When you see a symbol like the following, PN PN PN PN, it means that this proper noun consists of four words. Try to write this story during class time, and do not turn to page 32 for the original ad until you have finished.

5 In activity 4 you worked with an ad that was almost complete—it lacked only a number of nouns. In this activity you are going to do the opposite. We'll give you the nouns and let you make the ad. The following common nouns are the only ones used in a popular ad:

scent, sea, scent, women, men, sea, wave

Divide the class into groups before you begin

"You're a disgrace to the CN," they said as they tore the CNP from my CN.

"Good-bye PN"

My name was PN PN PN PN. But my fellow CNP in the PN PN PN called me "PN". I can still hear their CNP as they pointed to the shaving CNP that decorated my face like CNP of CN. And then that blackest of black days...I was drummed out of the PN. "You're a CN, PN", they said as they tore the CNP from my CNP. I wandered alone beneath the desert CNP, pondering my CN. Suddenly, at an CN, a mysterious CN slipped me a PN Techmatic® CN. I turned the CN to adjust it to my own individual CN and CN. I discovered that instead of CNP with sharp CNP that can cut and nick my CN, there's a continuous CN CN. All safely enclosed in a CN so I will never have to touch a sharp CN again. And I even noticed the different CN of the Techmatic...the CN, the CN. And I knew I would always get a smooth, safe CN.

I was restored to my CN with CN and became known as "PN of PN". And as long as there is a PN Techmatic... no CN will ever again call me "PN".

With PN TECHMATIC it's good-bye PN.

©The PN Company, PN, PN .

working on the following activities.

a Examine the nouns carefully and decide on the kind of product you think they are advertising.

b Give it a name. (A good one — one that will sell.)

c Design the ad. Roughly sketch some visual material and then write copy making use of the nouns in the list.

d The successful ad is the one that commands our attention. Make sure that yours is an attention grabber. (HINT: Why not try a clever play on words?)

e When you have finished, compare your ad with the ones from the other groups. Note the similarities and differences. Then, turn to page 33 for the original.

6 Sometimes we make statements consisting of an abstract noun and a clarifying detail: "Happiness is a warm puppy"; "Love is never having to say you're sorry." In the following newspaper column, Gary Lautens defines "middle-aged happiness." Following his example, write your own column defining one of the following:

teen-age happiness, love, security, jealousy, fear, success, popularity

Positive thinking can work wonders for middle-aged

Gary Lautens

Middle-aged people don't expect as much from life as the young, or the old.

In fact . . .

Middle-aged happiness is having enough hair to cover the bald spot.

Middle-aged happiness is a brother-in-law who makes less than you.

Middle-aged happiness is waking up in the morning and not seeing your name in the obituary column.

Middle-aged happiness is being first one home from the party.

Middle-aged happiness is finding out your wife's old boy friend wears dentures.

Middle-aged happiness is receiving a scented letter addressed, "To the householder."

Middle-aged happiness is discovering a dessert you like with 12 calories.

Middle-aged happiness is being recognized at the school reunion.

Middle-aged happiness is a hammock that swings and a daughter who doesn't.

Middle-aged happiness is finding out the sharp pain in your chest is only the tag left in your shirt by the laundry.

Middle-aged happiness is having a friend who can't give up cigarettes either.

Middle-aged happiness is missing the promotion at the office, but not very much.

Middle-aged happiness is remembering where you parked the car.

Middle-aged happiness is a wife who, when you leave for that second honeymoon in Paris, remembers to pack the prune juice.

Middle-aged happiness is playing golf with somebody else's boss, and winning.

Middle-aged happiness is finding the chocolate with the soft center.

Middle-aged happiness is a $9 refund check from the income tax department.

Middle-aged happiness is having a varicose vein where it doesn't show.

Middle-aged happiness is finding grass stains on the knees of your son's trousers, not in his pockets.

Middle-aged happiness is settling for a tattle-tale gray wedding for your daughter.

Middle-aged happiness is going to the golf course where your breadth comes in short pants.

Middle-aged happiness is discovering you can't see because you're wearing your wife's glasses.

Middle-aged happiness is a passionate kiss on the forehead.

"You're a disgrace to the regiment," they said as they tore the stripes from my arm.
"Good-bye NICK"

My name was Pierre Ettienne La Rogue. But my fellow officers in the French Foreign Legion called me, "Nick." I can still hear their jeers as they pointed to the shaving nicks that decorated my face like medals of dishonor. And then that blackest of black days—I was drummed out of the Legion. "You're a disgrace, Nick," they said as they tore the stripes from my arms.

I wandered alone beneath the desert stars, pondering my fate. Suddenly, at an oasis, a mysterious bedouin slipped me a Gillette Techmatic® razor. I turned the lever to adjust it to my own individual face and beard. I discovered that instead of blades with sharp corners that can cut and nick my face, there's a continuous razor band. All safely enclosed in a cartridge so I will never have to touch a sharp edge again. And I even noticed the different feel of the Techmatic...the lightness, the balance. And I knew I would always get a smooth, safe shave.

I was restored to my regiment with honor and became known as "Pierre of Pakistan." And as long as there is a Gillette Techmatic... no man will ever again call me "Nick."

With **Gillette TECHMATIC**
it's good-bye Nick

©The Gillette Company, Boston, Mass.

32

Scent from the sea.

Wind Drift® After Shave
and Cologne.
The clean, refreshing
scent for women
who love men
who love the sea.
It's like splashing on
a wave after he
shaves.

33

SOME USAGE PROBLEMS WITH NOUNS

ADVICE, ADVISE
"Advice" is a noun; "advise" a verb.

The Premier asked for the *advice* of his wife.
Men should do what their wives *advise*.

EFFECT, AFFECT
"Effect" may be a noun or a verb. As a noun it means "result" or "consequence." As a verb it means "to bring about, to achieve, to produce."

The *effect* of the new legislation was dramatic.
He plans to *effect* many changes in the housing laws.

"Affect" may be used only as a verb, meaning either "to influence" or "to make a pretense of."

Moonlight always *affects* me.
The new chairman *affected* an English accent.

KIND, SORT
These words are singular nouns and should be preceded by singular modifiers.

I like this *kind* of joke. (not: I like these kind of jokes.)
This *sort* of person is helpful. (not: These sort of people are helpful.)

PRINCIPAL, PRINCIPLE
"Principal" may be used as a noun or an adjective, meaning "chief" or "chief official." "Principle" is used as a noun meaning "basic law" or "fundamental truth."

The *principal* factor in his success was his determination.
Since his youth, he had wanted to become a high school *principal*.
He believed in the *principle* that all men are created equal.

NOUN-VERB AGREEMENT

1   Compound subjects are usually plural.

The two boys and their parents *are* in the office.
A pen and pencil *were* found in the corridor.

However, there is one exception to this rule.

When the compound subject refers to a single person or thing, or to two or more objects considered as a unit, it is followed by a singular verb.

My best friend and companion *has* left me. (One person was both friend and companion.)
The chairman and principal shareholder *is* Mr. Taylor.

2   When an element is added to the subject by the use of such expressions as "besides," "as well

as," "in addition to," the number of the subject is not changed.

Your mother, as well as my brother and his friends, *is* coming to our show tonight.
The increase in the cost of salaries, together with all the other expenses, *has* caused our taxes to rise.

3 A collective noun is singular when referring to a group as a unit but plural when referring to the members of a group individually.

Our class *was* dismissed early today. (The class is thought of here as a unit or group.)
The graduating class had *their* pictures taken yesterday. (The individual members of the class are referred to.)
The herd *was* seen at the water hole.
The herd *were* scattering in various directions.
The committee held *its* first meeting today.
The committee *were* divided in *their* responses to the news.

4 Most nouns which are plural in form but singular in meaning take singular verbs.

The news from the Middle East *is* good.
A million dollars *is* far too much.
Linguistics *is* the scientific study of language.

Some nouns are considered plural except when used after "pair."

His trousers *were* bought ten years ago.
An old pair of trousers *is* a necessity in his job.
The scissors *are* old and dull.
That pair of scissors *is* very expensive.

5 After a compound subject joined by "or," "nor," "either . . . or," "neither . . . nor," the verb agrees with the nearer part of the subject.

Either the man or his wife *is* guilty.
Neither the parents nor their son *has* arrived.
Neither the son nor his parents *have* arrived.

6 When a sentence begins with the introductory expletive (filler) "there" or "here," the number of the verb is determined by the subject which follows.

There *were* many errors in his examination.
There *was* a short intermission after the first act.
Here *is* something for you to remember.
Here *are* the only things I own.

7 A verb agrees with its subject, not its subjective completion.

Wine, women, and song *are* his main occupation.
His main occupation *is* wine, women, and song.
Our main concern *was* the many black flies in the area.
The black flies in the area *were* our main concern.

DISCOVERING VERBS (TRANSITIVE, INTRANSITIVE, AND LINKING VERBS)

For each of these pictures, write one simple sentence which describes the main action shown there.

Write some of the sentences on the chalkboard and circle the nouns in each sentence. These name people and objects, as you know. Now underline the words you have used to describe what the nouns are doing. List them. Add to the list any words used by other members of the class to describe what the nouns are doing. What do these words have in common? How do they differ from nouns? The general name for each of these words is *verb*. Specifically, each is a *transitive verb*.

Now look at the following pictures.

36

The lady is winking.

The actor was shouting.

The man fell.

Write on the chalkboard the sentence given here for each picture. Once again, circle the nouns. Underline the words you have used to describe what the nouns are doing and list them separately on the chalkboard. What do these words have in common with each other? What do they have in common with the transitive verbs used in the first set of pictures? How do they differ? These verbs are called *intransitive verbs*.

37

Now examine the following pictures and captions.

What are the verbs in each of the picture captions? How are these verbs similar to each other? How do they differ from transitive verbs? How are they similar? How do they differ from intransitive verbs? These verbs are called *linking verbs*.

We were a famous group.

I am a singer.

He seems puzzled.

Notice that in the sentences with transitive verbs a subject ("men," "boy," "man") was doing something ("tripped," "kisses," "bites") to someone ("lady," "girl," "dog"). The recipient of the action in each of these sentences is called the *direct object* (O). The following pattern indicates that a subject is performing an action on an object.

SV$_T$O (pattern 1)

The reporter hits the table.

S   V$_T$ O

A pattern 1 sentence must contain a subject, a verb and an object; it may, however, contain other elements in addition to these.

The men tripped the lady.
The young men tripped the old lady.
The foolish young men tripped the kind old lady.
Six foolish young men tripped the kind old lady from the Probation Office.
Early in the afternoon, six foolish young men tripped the kind old lady from the Probation Office.

In pattern 2 sentences, the intransitive verb is complete in itself; it does not require an object. Its pattern indicates that a subject is performing an action.

SVi (pattern 2)

The reporter is crying.

S   Vi

Pattern 2 sentences may also contain other elements.

Notice that, although an intransitive verb may be modified, it does not require a word to complete it.

The actor was shouting.
The enraged actor was shouting loudly.
The enraged actor was shouting loudly at the end of the show.
Still on the stage, the enraged actor was shouting loudly at the end of the show because he had missed the curtain call.

Pattern 3 sentences are similar to pattern 1 sentences in that the verbs in both require a word to complete them. Transitive verbs require an object; linking verbs require a subjective completion. The linking verb does not express action. It simply joins the subject to a word which completes it (C).

SV$_L$C (pattern 3)

We were a group.
We were a famous group.
We were a famous group of singers.
We were a famous group of singers from Britain.

The *subjective completion* is a word which completes the verb and refers back to the subject. It may be a noun, as in the example above, a pronoun, or an adjective.

It was hers.
He seems puzzled.

Notice that a linking verb *must* have another word to complete it.

The reporter became Superman.

S   V$_L$ C

Transitive (pattern 1)

The men tripped the lady.
The boy kisses the girl.
The man bites the dog.

SV$_T$O

Intransitive (pattern 2)

The lady is winking.
The man fell.
The actor was shouting.

SV$_i$

Linking (pattern 3)

I am a singer.
We were a famous group.
He seems puzzled.

SV$_L$C

---

1 Bring to class pictures similar to those on pages 36 to 38.

Divide the class into groups according to the instructions of your teacher. Within each group, work together to write sentences as captions for each of your pictures. Decide whether the main verb in each caption is transitive, intransitive or linking. Then read your group's captions to the rest of the class and explain your classification of verbs.

2 Some verbs may be transitive, intransitive, or linking, depending on how they are used in a sentence. We may say, for instance:

Algernon tastes the tea. (pattern 1)

This is a pattern 1 sentence and "tastes" is a transitive verb taking the direct object "tea." But if we say,

The tea tastes good. (pattern 3)

then the sentence is pattern 3 and "tastes" is a linking verb taking as its completion the adjective "good." Suppose, however, that the man tasting the tea in the first example is a tea-taster employed by a tea company. His sense of taste must be acute. To indicate that his taste buds are very sensitive, we may say:

Algernon tastes well. (pattern 2)

This is a pattern 2 sentence and "tastes" here is an intransitive verb.

Now imagine that Algernon is sent on a special mission by his company to jungle country and is captured by cannibals. The cannibal chief says:

Algernon tastes good!

What sentence pattern has the chief used? What kind of verb is "tastes" in this sentence? Why?

Compose three sentences for each of the following verbs. Each verb must be used as a transitive, intransitive, and linking verb.

grow, smell, feel, turn, sound

SMIDGENS

Verbs, like nouns, may be identified by certain grammatical features: inflection, signal words, and word order.

INFLECTION OF VERBS

Verbs are the only words in our language that can show a change in time by inflecting. We can show the difference, for instance, between the present and the past by changing the form of the verb:

walk—walked   sing—sang   throw—threw

The standard form of a verb, the form you see first if you look up the verb in a dictionary, is called the base form: "dance," "jump," "run," "sing," "do," "go." In addition to the base form, most verbs have four other forms: the present tense form, the past tense form, the present participle form, and the past participle form. (These are called the *principal parts* of a verb.)

The first two verbs in the list below, "dance" and "jump," are *regular verbs*. The others are *irregular verbs*. A verb is regular when it inflects in the following way:

"s" or "es" in the simple present: walks, washes
"ed" in the simple past: walked, washed
"ing" in the present participle: walking, washing
"ed" in the past participle: walked, washed

Most verbs in English are regular. In fact, the pattern of regular verbs is like a magnet tending to pull in irregular ones. The verb "heave" is a good example. Formerly, its past tense was "hove"; this form has been replaced today by the more regular "heaved." Irregular verbs are a closed class; that is, no new ones are being added to the language. Regular verbs, however, are an open class. When a new verb is coined, its principal parts are formed in the regular manner. What are the principal parts, for instance, of "computerize" and "skyjack"? What are some other new verbs that have recently come into use? Are they regular or irregular?

The language of young children provides us with a good example of our natural tendency to make verbs regular. The young child learns the system of regular verbs fairly early in his language development. After hearing many regular verbs being used, he learns to add "ed" for the

PRESENT	PAST	PRESENT PARTICIPLE	PAST PARTICIPLE
He (She) dances.	danced	(is) dancing	(has) danced
He (She) jumps.	jumped	(is) jumping	(has) jumped
He (She) runs.	ran	(is) running	(has) run
He (She) sings.	sang	(is) singing	(has) sung
He (She) does.	did	(is) doing	(has) done
He (She) goes.	went	(is) going	(has) gone

43

simple past and past participle forms: "walked,"
"talked," "washed," "looked," "jumped,"
"skipped." But with irregular verbs he finds
that he must memorize many of the forms because they don't seem to follow logical rules:
"ate," "sang," "ran," "went," "drank," "threw,"
"saw." Usually he learns the forms of common
verbs like "do," "go," "eat," "sing" and "see"
because he hears them so often. But quite often,
in his initial attempts to form the past tense of
these verbs, he tries to apply the system of
regular verbs to them and produces sentences
like the following:

"Daddy, you hurted me."
"Yesterday, I goed to the store."
"Billy throwed me the ball."
"They teached us to count at nursery school last
week."

Show how, in each of these sentences, the
young child is acting very logically. Bring to class
any examples of this kind of manipulation of verb
forms you hear from your own younger brothers
or sisters.

SIGNAL WORDS—VERB MARKERS

Just as there are determiners to signal the presence of nouns in a sentence, so too are there
signal words which point to the presence of
verbs—structure words called *auxiliaries.* The
main auxiliaries in English are forms of the
verbs "be," "have," and "do." In addition, there
is a group of auxiliaries known as "modals":
"must," "will/would," "shall/should," "can/
could," "may/might." Notice how auxiliaries
function as verb markers in these sentences.

I *am* working today.
They *had* finished their work early.
Did she complete her homework?
He *must* buy that record.
You *will* succeed if you try hard.

Test Frame for Verbs

We saw on page 18 how test frames could be
used to help determine what part of speech a
word is. In the following test frame, we use the
principle of word order and the structure word
"let's" to help us determine whether or not a
word is a verb.

Let's_____(it).

To determine whether a word is a verb, try it in
the blank space. If the resulting sentence sounds
natural, then the word is a verb. The word "it" is
in parentheses because it does not have to be
used for all verbs. Certain verbs, however, will
fit only if "it" is used. Test the following words to
see if they are verbs: "buy," "run," "because,"
"energetic," "eat," "and," "go." Notice that this
test frame will not work for all the principal parts
of a verb, but it will work for any base form.

activities

1 In the following newspaper account, some old-
fashioned verb forms, rarely heard in modern
English, are used. Make a list of these verbs and
opposite each write the modern equivalent.
What has happened to each of the older forms?
What "rule" of language change seems to be in
evidence here?

Rolls Robbery Reported

(NP) Police are investigating a robbery reported by Mrs. Abigail Murgotroyd, chairperson of the Muddletown Annual Home Baking Contest. Mrs. Murgotroyd, a well-known socialite, has baken her own bread and rolls for years. She reported yesterday that two young ruffians clomb her fence and stole a pan of rolls from her kitchen window. "Not only did they steal them," said Mrs. Murgotroyd, "but one of the little devils actually hove a roll at me as I chased them. Fortunately, I saw it as it glode through the air, and ducked. I yelled for them to come back, but neither of the young scoundrels durst face me." The investigation continues.

2 The following story is an interview between a reporter and a very colorful sports announcer. The announcer, Infield Ingersoll, has applied his own set of rules for regular and irregular verbs. As you read the interview, try to figure out Infield's system of verb formation.

Who Flang That Ball?

My assignment was to interview Infield Ingersoll, one-time shortstop for the Wescosville Wombats and now a radio sports announcer. Dizzy Dean, Red Barber and other sportscasters had taken back seats since the colorful Ingersoll had gone on the air. The man had practically invented a new language.

"I know just what you're gonna ask," Infield began. "You wanna know how come I use all them ingrammatical expressions like 'He swang at a high one.' You think I'm illitrut."

"No, indeed," I said. Frankly, I *had* intended to ask him what effect he thought his extraordinary use of the King's English might have on future generations of radio listeners.

But a gleam in Infield's eyes when he said "illitrut" changed my mind. "What I'd really like to get," I said, "is the story of how you left baseball and became a sportscaster."

Infield looked pleased. "Well," he said, "it was the day us Wombats plew the Pink Sox . . ."

"Plew the Pink Sox?" I interrupted. "Don't you mean played?"

Infield's look changed to disappointment. "Slay, slew. Play, plew. What's the matter with that?"

"Slay is an irregular verb," I pointed out.

"So who's to say what's regular or irregular? English teachers! Can an English teacher bat three hundred?"

He paused belligerently, and then went on. "What I'm trying to do is easify the languish. I make all regular verbs irregular. Once they're all irregular, then it's just the same like they're all regular. That way I don't gotta stop and think."

He had something there. "Go on with your story," I said.

"Well, it was the top of the fifth, when this Sox batter wang out a high pop fly. I raught for it."

"Raught?"

"Past tense of verb to reach. Teach, taught. Reach,—"

"Sorry," I said. "Go ahead."

"Anyhow I raught for it, only the sun blound me."

"You mean blinded?"

"Look," Infield said patiently, "you wouldn't say a pitcher winded up, would you? So there I was, blound by the sun, and the ball just nuck the tip of my glove—that's nick, nuck; same congregation as stick, stuck. But luckily I caught it just as it skam the top of my shoe."

"Skam? Could that be the past tense of to skim?"

"Yeah, yeah, same as swim, swam. You want this to be a English lesson or you wanna hear my story?"

"Your story please, Mr. Ingersoll."

"Okay. Well, just then the umpire cell, 'Safe!' Naturally I was surprise. Because I caught that fly, only the ump cell the runner safe."

"Cell is to call as fell is to fall, I suppose?" I inquired.

"Right. Now you're beginning to catch on." Infield regarded me happily as if there was now some hope for me. "So I yold at him, 'Robber! That decision smold!'"

"Yell, yold. Smell, smold," I mumbled. "Same idea as tell, told."

Infield rumbled on, "I never luck that umpire anyway."

"Hold it!" I cried. I finally had tripped this backhand grammarian. "A moment ago, you used nuck as the past for nick, justifying it by the verb to stick. Now you use luck as a verb. Am I to assume by this that luck is the past tense of to lick?"

"Luck is past for like. To like is a regular irregular verb of which there are several such as strike, struck. Any further questions or should I go on?"

"Excuse me," I said, "you were saying you never luck that umpire."

"And neither did the crowd. Everyone thrould at my courage. I guess I better explain thrould," Infield said thoughtfully. "Thrould comes from thrill just like would comes from will. Got that? Now to get back to my story: 'Get off the field, you bum, and no back talk!' the umpire whoze."

"Whoze?"

"He had asthma," Infield pointed out patiently.

I saw through it instantly. Wheeze, whoze. Freeze, froze.

"And with those words, that ump invote disaster. I swang at him and smeared him with a hard right that lood square on his jaw."

"Lood? Oh, I see—Stand, stood. Land, lood— it lood on his jaw."

"Sure. He just feld up and went down like a light. As he reclone on the field, he pept at me out of his good eye."

"Now wait. What's this pept?" I asked.

"After you sleep, you've did what?" Infield inquired.

"Why, slept—oh, he peeped at you, did he?"

46

"You bet he pept at me. And in that peep I saw it was curtains for me in the league henceforward. So I beat him to it and just up and quat."

"Sit, sat. Quit—well, that gets you out of baseball," I said. "Only you still haven't told me how you got to be on radio and television."

"I guess that'll have to wait," Infield said, "on account I gotta hurry now to do a broadcast."

As he shade my hand good-by, Infield grun and wank at me.

W. F. Miksch

a In this story, Infield Ingersoll says that he is trying to "easify the languish." What is the system he uses? Is he successful?

b How is his system similar to that of a young child? How does it differ?

c Infield Ingersoll explains most of his expressions for the interviewer, but he does leave some to the imagination. Using the same procedure as he does, explain the italicized words in the following sentences from the story:

• What I'm trying to do is *easify* the languish.
• Well, it was the top of the fifth, when this Sox batter *wang* out a high pop fly.
• Naturally I was *surprose*.
• And with those words, that ump *invote* disaster.
• Sure. He just *feld* up and went down like a light.
• As he *reclone* on the field, he pept at me out of his good eye.
• As he *shade* my hand good-by, Infield *grun* and *wank* at me.

d Although this is a humorous interview, it does deal with a problem that troubles many speakers of English: our verb system. As you have seen, Infield tries to make all regular verbs irregular. Many modern speakers try just the opposite technique: to make all irregular verbs regular. See if there is any confusion in your class about the following verbs. Which form of the verb in parentheses would you use in each of the following sentences?

1 Yesterday he_____into the pool from the high board. (dive)

2 I have_____three bottles of pop today. (drink)

3 He has_____his lunch to school today. (bring)

4 I have_____in Lake Ontario twice. (swim)

5 What time do you wish to be_____? (awake)

VERB SUFFIXES AND PREFIXES

In addition to having characteristic inflectional suffixes, verbs also possess typical derivational suffixes. Write the required verbs (derived from the word in parentheses) in the following sentences:

1 We had to_____too many lines last year. (memory)

2 Conservationists hope to_____our water supply. (pure)

3 Where did that word_____? (origin)

4 We must add ink to_____the mixture. (dark)

5 He hopes to_____in criminal law. (special)

6 Our class tried to_____a scene from *Julius Caesar*. (drama)

7 Can you_____the others in the group? (identity)

List the verb suffixes that you have used to form verbs from the words in parentheses. For each suffix write five other verbs and use each of these in a sentence. Which verb suffix is most commonly used today to form verbs?

Verbs are formed not only by adding suffixes to root words but also by placing prefixes before the roots. The most common verb prefixes are *en* and *be* as in "engulf" and "befriend." Write three other verbs with the prefix "en" and three with the prefix "be" and use each of them in a sentence.

In the following list we see some of the other common verb prefixes. What does each prefix mean?

"de": deactivate, decode, de-escalate, delouse, defoliate

"dis": dislike, disagree, disappear, disperse, dismember

"mis": misbehave, mistrust, miscalculate, misinform, misfire, misspell, misstate, misshape, misspend

"re": repay, replace, refund, restate, rewrite

"pre": prearrange, precook, prepay, prepare, preview

Note:
You may have spelling difficulties with words like "misspell," which is made up of the prefix "mis" and the verb "spell." What simple pattern can you observe in the use of prefixes which will help in your spelling of words like these?

USING VERBS EFFECTIVELY

Your knowledge about verbs, just like your knowledge of grammar in general, is useless unless you apply it. If you make a conscious effort to *use* verbs effectively, you can improve your writing significantly. The effective use of appropriate verbs can transform dull, pedestrian material into vigorous, colorful writing. Try to be more selective and imaginative in your use of verbs. Obviously, improving your verb usage is not enough by itself, but it is a step in the right direction.

Verbs like "say," "walk," "run" are adequate to convey meaning. They are limited, however, because they are so general. They tell *what* was happening but they do not shed much light on *how* it was being done. Verbs like "shout," "mutter," "grumble," "amble," "saunter," "stride," "trot," "dash," "canter" are not only more precise but also more colorful. Our language is rich with such verb synonyms. Don't be satisfied with just any verb. Develop the habit of searching for the exact one to fit your sentence.

Of course, it's easy to advise you to "search" for the exact word. But where do you look if you can't think of an alternative? Sometimes a dictionary will help. Better than a dictionary, however, is one of the most valuable sources of words for any writer: Roget's *Thesaurus* (or any book of synonyms). If you don't own a copy, buy a paperback edition. It contains a valuable supply of synonyms and related words and phrases for practically any word you use.

Suppose, for example, you are writing an essay about a humorous incident. You realize that you have repeated the verb "laugh" too often, but you can't think of other verbs to substitute for it. You know there are others, but your mind is blank. Turning to your handy *Thesaurus,* and return to your essay. Perhaps a following: titter, giggle; chuckle, chortle; cackle, crow; snicker, snigger, snort; guffaw, horselaugh; roar, cachinnate; split one's sides, laugh oneself sick. Now you have a choice. There may be two or three familiar synonyms that fit exactly into the context of your essay. If such is the case, you thank Roget, close your *Thesaurus* and return to your essay. Perhaps a word is given ("snigger") which you recognize but whose meaning you are not positive about. Then you have to check it in a dictionary. Other words you will reject immediately because they do not fit the tone of your essay. Don't become the kind of writer who discovers a word like "cachinnate" and uses it only because it is a "big word." Its use would probably be inappropriate, if not phony and pretentious, for any essay you would be writing. (It means "to laugh loudly," by the way. Have you ever seen it or heard it before?) Other expressions like "split one's sides" or " horselaugh" might be too informal for your essay. But the advantage of a *Thesaurus* is that it at least has given you a choice of words where none existed before.

activities

1 In the following lists, synonyms for the common verbs "eat," "sing," and "grab" are given. Imagine a situation where each of the words could be appropriately used (a separate situation for each word). Write a sentence for each word, indicating after your sentence the physical description of the person or thing performing

the action and the circumstances under which it was performed. Have various students read their sentences aloud and let the rest of the class try to guess the physical descriptions and circumstances.

EAT: consume, devour, gobble, munch, nibble, feed one's face, stuff, gulp, crunch
SING: croon, vocalize, warble, chirp, intone, serenade, belt out, lull, chant
GRAB: seize, take, grasp, snatch, clutch, throttle, clasp, grip

2 Play the "Vigorous Verbs" game. In this game we try to use precise and forceful verbs to indicate the action that "Mary" is performing. For instance, our first sentence is:

Mary *said* that she was tired.

Rather than using the general verb "said," we expand the sentence by substituting a more vivid verb and adding some details.

Mary *whispered* that she was tired as she quietly closed the door.
Mary *muttered* that she was tired as her mother tried to wake her.
Mary *screamed* that she was tired and begged her brother to turn down his stereo.
Mary *gasped* that she was tired as we neared the top of the mountain.
Mary *whined* that she was tired and wanted to sleep before the exam.
Mary *shrieked* that she was tired and would like to rest.
Mary *complained* that she was tired and would finish her homework in the morning.

a Make up some more "Mary said" sentences using the following verbs. For each sentence, have a student say "I am tired" in a way that will illustrate the verb used. For example, students will have to dramatize the action of Mary murmuring, shouting, hissing, and sighing the sentence "I am tired."

murmur, shout, hiss, sigh, growl, snap, snarl, grunt, moan, wail

b Follow the directions in (a) for the following sentence.

Mary *went* to the door.

Use the following verbs:

rush, stagger, shuffle, strut, glide, stumble, race, bounce, stride, dart

3 Imagine that you have been asked to write an article for a popular magazine for boat owners. In your article you must describe the way various boats approach the dock. A canoe, of course, would "glide in." A tugboat might "chug" into dock. What verbs would you use to describe the movement of a yacht? an ocean liner? a rowboat? a sailboat?

Write a paragraph describing the action of one of the people or things in each of the following sections. Concentrate on using exact, specific, colorful verbs.

a an animal moving through the jungle: lion, monkey, snake, gorilla, elephant, giraffe, gazelle, panther

b an athlete in motion: wrestler, boxer, figure skater, tennis player, hockey player, fencer,

football player, roller derby skater

c an automobile being parked: Volkswagen, Cadillac, Porsche, Jeep, station wagon

d a person eating: baseball fan at a game; society matron eating lunch; young boy eating his final pie in a pie-eating competition; hungry man eating a ripe watermelon; a librarian eating celery in a crowded library

4 Write a letter to your best friend. In your letter describe one of the following. Once again, concentrate on your verbs.

a a train pulling into a station

b a parade in progress

c a plane landing

d a computer

e any machine in operation

5 Imagine that you are a radio announcer. You have been assigned to "cover" one of the events illustrated by the photographs on this page and the next. Write out a commentary describing the action for one of these events.

ACTION VERBS VS. LINKING VERBS

Practically all the verbs you have been using in the previous activities are action verbs, transitive or intransitive. Action verbs enable you to inject life into weak sentences. They help you vitalize your sentences with color, sound, action, and feeling. Unfortunately, many inexperienced writers tend to neglect them and rely on the more lifeless linking verbs. A student covering a football game for his school newspaper could write:

The crowd was very angry.

The verb "was," a form of the linking verb "to be," is grammatically correct here. But is it effective? Couldn't the writer have found a more forceful verb to tell us whether the crowd "thundered" its displeasure, or "erupted" with anger, or "seethed" or "raged" or even "boiled"?

There is an appropriate use for linking verbs in our language. They enable us to name and identify people, things, feelings. But most of them function simply as an "equals sign."

"Washington, D.C. is the nation's capital" means "Washington, D.C.=the nation's capital." As you know from the formula for pattern 3 sentences (S V_L C), linking verbs are not complete in themselves. They must be followed by a completion which gives meaning to the sentence. By themselves they are inadequate. If your writing has been criticized because it lacks vitality or color, examine the verbs you have been using. Make sure that you are not relying on linking verbs to do the work of action verbs. When Marshall McLuhan described a popular young disc jockey, he could have written:

Dave Mickie was very energetic.

Fortunately he did not. He chose his verbs more carefully and wrote:

Dave Mickie alternately soars, groans, swings, sings, solos, intones and scampers, always reacting to his own actions.

From *Understanding Media,* by Marshall McLuhan

activities

1 Read the poem on page 54 silently. Then have two students read it aloud. Student A reads the first two lines of each stanza; student B reads the last two. Student A reads the entire last stanza. After the poem has been read and discussed in class, write down the important verbs and verb forms used in each stanza. How do the gradual changes in action depicted by these verbs help you understand what happened in the poem? What is the theme of this poem?

Ballad

O what is that sound which so thrills the ear
    Down in the valley drumming, drumming?
Only the scarlet soldiers, dear,
    The soldiers coming.

O what is that light I see flashing so clear
    Over the distance brightly, brightly?
Only the sun on their weapons, dear,
    As they step lightly.

O what are they doing with all that gear;
    What are they doing this morning, this morning?
Only the usual manœuvres, dear,
    Or perhaps a warning.

O why have they left the road down there;
    Why are they suddenly wheeling, wheeling?
Perhaps a change in the orders, dear;
    Why are you kneeling?

O haven't they stopped for the doctor's care;
    Haven't they reined their horses, their horses?
Why, they are none of them wounded, dear,
    None of these forces.

O is it the parson they want, with white hair;
    Is it the parson, is it, is it?
No, they are passing his gateway, dear,
    Without a visit.

O it must be the farmer who lives so near,
    It must be the farmer, so cunning, cunning;
They have passed the farm already, dear,
    And now they are running.

O where are you going? Stay with me here.
    Were the vows you swore me deceiving, deceiving?
No, I promised to love you, dear.
    But I must be leaving.

O it's broken the lock and splintered the door,
    O it's the gate where they're turning, turning;
Their feet are heavy on the floor
    And their eyes are burning.

W. H. Auden

2 a Spend a few minutes reading the following poem. Then have a volunteer read the poem dramatically to the class. Divide the class into groups according to the instructions of your teacher. Each group is to examine the poem carefully, stanza by stanza, pick out the nonsense verbs and discuss what they might possibly mean. Obviously there is no one "meaning" for each of them. But discuss with the other members of your group what they *might* mean and write down your possibilities. When you have finished, compare your ideas with those of the other groups.

Jabberwocky

'Twas brillig, and the slithy toves
   Did gyre and gimble in the wabe;
All mimsy were the borogoves,
   And the mome raths outgrabe.

"Beware the Jabberwock, my son!
   The jaws that bite, the claws that catch!
Beware the Jubjub bird, and shun
   The frumious Bandersnatch!"

He took his vorpal sword in hand:
   Long time the manxome foe he sought —
So rested he by the Tumtum tree,
   And stood awhile in thought.

And, as in uffish thought he stood,
   The Jabberwock, with eyes of flame,
Came whiffling through the tulgy wood,
   And burbled as it came!

One, two! One, two! And through and through
   The vorpal blade went snicker-snack!
He left it dead, and with its head
   He went galumphing back.

"And hast thou slain the Jabberwock?
   Come to my arms, my beamish boy!
O frabjous day! Callooh! Callay!"
   He chortled in his joy.

'Twas brillig, and the slithy toves
   Did gyre and gimble in the wabe:
All mimsy were the borogoves,
   And the mome raths outgrabe.

Lewis Carroll

b Now try making up some of your own non-sense verbs. Each group should make up one for each of the following. When you have finished, compare yours with those from the other groups.

—to eat peanuts noiselessly ("to smunch"? "to chunkle"?)
—to exhale through your nose
—to trip someone with a skipping rope
—to drink with your mouth full
—to drive on the highway at 20 miles per hour in the passing lane
—to rub noses with someone of the opposite sex
—to scratch your ear with your forearm

3 Read silently the poem below about a railroad train. Then have someone read it aloud to the class. List the verbs used by the poet, in order, on the chalkboard. To what is she comparing the train? Show how the verbs used describe the movement of the train? What is her attitude toward it?

4 Try your hand at writing poetry. Choose one of the people from the following list. Write down every verb you can think of in connection with that "person." Using some of these verbs to get you started, write a poem about him or her.

tramp, policeman, politician, popular singer, lumberjack, ballerina, athlete, old man, baby, comedian

I Like to See It Lap the Miles

I like to see it lap the miles,
And lick the valleys up,
And stop to feed itself at tanks;
And then, prodigious, step

Around a pile of mountains,
And, supercilious, peer
In shanties by the sides of roads;
And then a quarry pare

To fit its sides, and crawl between,
Complaining all the while
In horrid, hooting stanza:
Then chase itself downhill

And neigh like Boanerges;
Then, punctual as a star,
Stop—docile and omnipotent—
At its own stable door.

Emily Dickinson

SOME USAGE PROBLEMS WITH VERBS

ACCEPT, EXCEPT
The verb "accept" means "to receive," "to give an affirmative answer to." The verb "except" means "to exclude." "Except" as a preposition means "with the exclusion of," "but."

His enemies said that he *accepted* the bribe.
They *excepted* him from the invitation list.
All the writers *except* one believed him guilty.

BRING, TAKE
"Bring" means "come with" and indicates motion toward the speaker. "Take" means "go with" and indicates motion away from the speaker.

Bring me the groceries and *take* the empty carton back to the store.

DONE
The principal parts of the verb "do," are "do, did, done."

I *did* my homework last night. (not: I done my homework last night.)
I have *done* all my work this year. (not: I done all my work this year.)

DON'T
The third person singular form of the verb "do" is "does." In the negative it becomes "does not," or "doesn't."

She *doesn't* believe in witchcraft. (not: She don't believe in witchcraft.)
They *don't* want to come home.

HANGED, HUNG
Informally, "hanged" and "hung" are often used interchangeably. In formal usage "hanged" is preferred when referring to executions and "hung" when referring to the suspension of objects.

No one has been *hanged* for murder in the United States for many years.
The abstract painting was *hung* in the den.

IMPLY, INFER
A speaker or writer "implies"; a listener or reader "infers." "Imply" means "to hint or suggest"; "infer" means "to derive a conclusion."

The lecturer *implied* that the President was guilty.
The audience *inferred* from the speech that the President was guilty.

LEARN, TEACH
"To learn" means "to acquire knowledge"; "to teach" means "to impart or pass on knowledge."

He could not *learn* how to organize his time until Mr. Smothers *taught* him efficiency.

LIE, LAY
"Lie" is an intransitive verb meaning "to recline." Its principal parts are "lie, lay, lain." "Lay" is a transitive verb meaning "to place or put." Its principal parts are "lay, laid, laid."
to lie:
Yesterday he was tired and *lay* down for an hour.
After he had *lain* there for an hour, he got up.
Other people were *lying* on the beaches.
The logs have been *lying* there for years.
to lay:
Last week he *laid* bricks for the new house.
After he had *laid* the bricks, he started the roof.

They are *laying* the cornerstone for the new building today.

"Lie" (to tell an untruth) is an intransitive verb. Its principal parts are "lie, lied, lied."

LOSE, LOOSE
"Lose" is a verb meaning "to cease having," "to misplace." "Loose" is usually used as an adjective meaning "free, not tight." When it is used as a verb, "to loose" means "to set free."

That button is *loose*; be careful, you may *lose* it.

OF
The use of the preposition "of" is nonstandard when it is substituted for the verb "have" in such expressions as "could of," "may of," "might of," "must of," "ought to of," "would of."

Our team could *have* (may *have*, might *have*, must *have*, ought to *have*, would *have*) set a new record last year.

RISE, RAISE
"Rise" is an intransitive verb meaning "to move upward," "to get up." Its principal parts are "rise, rose, risen." "Raise" is a transitive verb meaning "to lift," "to grow." Its principal parts are "raise, raised, raised."

Yesterday he *rose* at six a.m.
He *raised* his hand in class twice this morning.

SIT, SET
"Sit" is an intransitive verb meaning "to be seated," "to rest." Its principal parts are "sit, sat, sat." "Set" is a transitive verb meaning "to place in position." Its principal parts are "set, set, set."

The beauty queen *sat* on her throne and cried. Last year's winner *set* the crown on her head.

"Set" also may be used as an intransitive verb. In this sense, the sun, a hen and concrete all *set*.

DISCOVERING ADJECTIVES

Divide the class into groups according to the instructions of your teacher. Read the ad on page 59 and discuss with the other members of your group possible words that could be inserted in the numbered blank spaces. Note that there are only five words missing; each word is repeated in the second half of the ad. After the group has agreed on its words, list them in your notebook.

After all the groups have completed their lists, write each list on the chalkboard. Discuss in class which words in each list are most appropriate for this ad. Make sure the words you choose are consistent with the artwork and with the "message" the copywriter is trying to convey about this product.

Now compare your words with the original ad, given on page 94. How close did you come? By examining the original words, we can easily see what qualities of this perfume the copywriter was stressing. Sum up in your own words, in one sentence, what this ad is telling you about the product. If your list of words differed from the original, discuss what "message" your ad conveyed.

The words you supplied are adjectives. What do they do in the ad? Try to write a definition of an adjective based on their function in this ad.

© Coty, New York

Why a boy gives a girl flowers.

He said he gave me flowers because flowers are __1__ and __2__.

He said he gave me flowers because they're something __3__ and __4__.

He said he gave me flowers because those are the things I am.

And I hope he's right, because that's what I try to be.

Everything __5__, the

way nature is.

Even with the perfume I wear.

Muguet des bois.
Which means "Flower of the Woods." And that's as __5__ as you can get.

Something __1__ and __2__, __3__ and __4__.

Muguet des bois by Coty

In the ad on page 59 we learned that flowers are (1) "soft," (2) "pretty," (3) "real," (4) "honest," and (5) "natural." Each of these adjectives gives us additional information about the noun "flowers." In this sense they "modify" the noun. The traditional definition of an adjective, "a word that modifies a noun or a pronoun," is helpful to us in recognizing adjectives—provided we realize that the definition is limited and does not refer to all adjectives, nor to all words that "modify" nouns. What is more helpful to us than a definition, however, is the examination of the same grammatical signals which operated for nouns and verbs: inflection, signal words, and word order.

INFLECTION

'Twas brillig and the slithy toves
  Did gyre and gimble in the wabe;
All mimsy were the borogoves,
  And the mome raths outgrabe.

Pick out four words from the first verse of Lewis Carroll's "Jabberwocky" that you would classify as adjectives. Discuss your choices with the rest of the class. Why did you pick each of these words? What clues helped you to identify them as adjectives? Now try inserting each of the four words you have chosen in the following test sentences, varying the form of your adjectives in each case to correspond to the particular sentence. For instance, if the adjective were "snorpy," you would write:

1 That creature on my desk is *snorpy*.
2 That creature on the floor is *snorpier*.
3 But that creature in the cage is the *snorpiest*.

Try each of your four words in these sentences:
1 That creature on my desk is_____.
2 That creature on the floor is_____.
3 But that creature in the cage is the_____.

These forms of the adjectives are called the *positive* ("snorpy"), the *comparative* ("snorpier"), and the *superlative* ("snorpiest") degrees. Practically all regular adjectives in English can be made comparative and superlative by either adding an inflectional ending or using certain structure words. What are the inflectional endings?

Even though you may have made occasional mistakes as a child ("She plays gooder than me," "My daddy is the bestest"), you probably experienced little trouble learning how to form the comparative and superlative of adjectives. The only problem with regular adjectives is figuring out which use inflectional endings ("er" and "est") and which use structure words ("more" and "most"). Nonsense words like the ones you experimented with can be useful in helping you discover the general patterns we follow in comparing adjectives. Your class probably argued about "brillig" and "mome." Should we say "brilliger" or "more brillig"? Is it "momest" or "most mome"? Perhaps there was more agreement about "slithy" and "mimsy" because these words seem similar to "holy" and "happy." See now if you can discover the "rules."

activities

1 Divide the class into groups according to the instructions of your teacher. Each group is to try

60

to discover the general pattern or principle for comparing adjectives by making a chart of the positive, comparative, and superlative forms of each adjective in the following list. When you have discovered a pattern, express it in the form of a "rule." After all the groups have finished, appoint one member from each to write his group's rule on the chalkboard. By discussing the strengths and weaknesses of each group's "rule," formulate a general rule for the comparison of adjectives.

wise	loyal	short
sad	pretty	simple
beautiful	cheap	ugly
comfortable	useful	famous
happy	fantastic	wild
terrible	unbelievable	busy
hard	tall	

2 As with many rules, there are exceptions. Make a chart in your notebook indicating the comparison of the following irregular adjectives: good, bad, little, far, many.

3 In the ad on this page the copywriter has depended largely on adjectives to convince potential buyers to purchase his product. Make two lists of adjectives: (a) those used to describe the noun "lips"; (b) those used to describe the colors of "Lip Gloss" available.

a Why is the comparative form used for all the adjectives in list (a)? Comment on the effectiveness of these adjectives. Do the same for list (b). Why did the copywriter not use an adjective like "delicious," "appealing," or "luscious" in list (a)?

b Only one adjective is repeated in this ad. Which one? Why is this particular adjective repeated and no other? Which verb is repeated? Why?
c Comment on the effectiveness of the following phrases used in the ad: "A new twist . . . ," "The Big Brush-On."

A new twist...

and you brush on glossier, wetter, neater, livelier, lovelier lips.
It's Elizabeth Arden's New Automatic Lip Gloss.
In clear, pink, tawny, currant.
Brush, brush, brush your lips to beautiful.

The Big Brush-On

Elizabeth Arden

DERIVATIONAL SUFFIXES

We use many different suffixes to form adjectives: some indicate only adjectives; others are used for adjectives and other parts of speech. Discover some of the most common adjective suffixes by completing the following sentences. Write on a sheet of paper the adjective that fits in the blank of the second sentence in each pair. The adjective must be formed from the italicized word in the first sentence of each pair. Underline the derivational suffix of each adjective you supply.

Example: John is my *friend*. He is a friend*ly* person.

1 His conversation sounded like a *book*. It was extremely_____.
2 He enjoys the *comfort* of his new bed. It is very_____.
3 There is much *danger* ahead. Our route is quite_____.
4 The admiral was a *hero*. His_____action was commended.
5 He has great *hope* for the future. The outlook is_____.
6 He has no *hope* for the future. The outlook is_____.
7 He always shows good *sense*. He is very _____.
8 The witness made no *response* to the question. He was not a_____witness.
9 Your stories will always *fascinate* me. You are a_____person.
10 She appeared to have the innocence of a *child*. This_____quality was very appealing.

Make a list of the suffixes you used. Write three adjectives for each suffix and use each in a sentence which clearly illustrates its meaning.

SIGNAL WORDS

There are no signal words that identify only adjectives. The common signalers, like "very," "quite," "rather," may be used with adjectives or adverbs. You can discover these signalers by substituting appropriate words for "very" in the sentence, "He is *very* happy."

He is_____happy.

Make a list of these words and indicate the ones which would be appropriate only for informal conversation.

In traditional grammar, words like "very," "quite," and "rather" are classified as adverbs because they modify adjectives or other adverbs. In more modern grammars, they are called *intensifiers* because they add to the weight or force of the words following them; they intensify the word that follows them.

Some words, such as "pretty," can be used both as intensifiers and also as adjectives. "Pretty" is an adjective in the sentence, "She is a pretty girl." It is used informally as an intensifier in the sentence, "That was a pretty good movie."

WORD ORDER

Adjectives commonly occur in two positions in English sentences: before nouns and after linking verbs.

The young man entered the arena. (The adjective "young" modifies the noun "man.")

The man seemed young. (The adjective "young" modifies the noun "man.")

Test Frame for Adjectives

Because these are the normal adjective positions, the following test frame applies for most adjectives.

The_____(noun) seemed very_____.

Here any word which fits both spaces is an adjective. "Young" is an adjective because we can say, "The *young* man seemed very *young*," but "hat" is not because we do not say, "The *hat* man seemed very *hat*."

Although the two positions indicated are the most common for adjectives, there are others where they occasionally occur. Consider the following sentence:

The boys, tired and hungry, returned home.

DISCOVERING ADVERBS

A few years ago a word game called "Tom Swifties" was very popular, especially among people who delighted in word play. The idea of the game was to create a humorous pun by the use of a word modifying the verb in a sentence about Tom Swift. For example:

"I'll have four hot dogs," said Tom *frankly*.

"I suppose you've drunk all the lemonade?" Tom asked *dryly*.

"Move to the rear of the ship," Tom requested *sternly*.

See if you can complete these "Tom Swifties":

"I had no trouble with my electrocardiogram," Tom said_____.

"You gave me two less than a dozen," Tom complained_____.

"Please pass the sugar," said Tom_____.

The words you supplied in the "Tom Swifty" sentences were adverbs. Each one described *how* Tom "said" or "complained." In this sense they "modified" these verbs. Adverbs can also combine with verbs to tell us *when* or *why* an action was done. Grammarians sometimes use the words "there," "then," and "thus" to test adverbs. In the three sets of sentences on page 64, we group the italicized adverbs in this manner. What question does each set of adverbs answer?

there — Adverbs of Place

The student rushed *outside.*
My dog ran *away.*
Let's go *out* tonight.
May we have the party *here?*

then — Adverbs of Time

Your essay is due *today.*
Sometimes we eat steak.
We *always* have hamburgers.
Give me the money *immediately.*

thus — Adverbs of Manner

He walked home *quickly.*
It is snowing *heavily.*
Suddenly he realized the answer.
We talked *quietly* in church.

Write sentences containing five other adverbs of place, adverbs of time, and adverbs of manner.

WORD ORDER

Examine the example sentences above. Do the adverbs occupy any single slot in the sentences, or do they occur in different positions? What conclusions can you draw about the position of adverbs in English sentences?

INFLECTION

Inflectional endings are not much help to us in identifying adverbs. Some take the same inflectional endings as adjectives to form the comparative and superlative degrees. Adverbs like "fast," "high," "late" make use of the "er" and "est" endings to show degree. Other adverbs, like "there," "then," "now," "here," cannot be compared. But most adverbs form their comparative and superlative degrees by using the structure words "more" and "most." Three common adverbs whose comparative and superlative are irregular are "well," "badly," and "far." What are the comparative and superlative forms of these adverbs?

DERIVATIONAL SUFFIXES

The "ly" ending is the one most commonly associated with adverbs. Most students immediately recognize words like "quickly," "correctly," and "frequently" as adverbs. But even though "ly" is a common adverb ending, we should not make the assumption that all words ending in "ly" are therefore adverbs.

Adverbs are usually formed from adjectives by adding the derivational suffix "ly."

ADJECTIVE	ADVERB
quick	quick*ly*
correct	correct*ly*
frequent	frequent*ly*

But when you add "ly" to a noun, the resulting part of speech is not an adverb, but an adjective.

NOUN	ADJECTIVE
friend	friend*ly*
ghost	ghost*ly*
coward	coward*ly*

Careful speakers and writers are very cautious about using adverbs formed with the suffix "wise." Although it is true that there are appropriate adverbs like "clockwise" and "lengthwise," people who care about their use of the language avoid constructions like the following:

Moneywise our government is in trouble.
(Our government needs money.)
Billy has no problem *ability wise,* but *work wise* he leaves something to be desired.
(Billy is smart, but lazy.)

Read what the *American Heritage Dictionary of the English Language* has to say about this suffix:

The practice of attaching *wise* to nouns, in the sense of *with reference to,* has become so closely associated with commercial jargon in the minds of many writers and speakers that it is dubious usage on any higher level. Resistance to such combinations is also strengthened by the tendency of some persons to form them indiscriminately and to overuse them. The following typical examples, often found in business writing and speech as an aid to conciseness, are termed unacceptable in general usage by 84 per cent of the Usage Panel: *Taxwise, it is an attractive arrangement. The report is not encouraging saleswise.*

SIGNAL WORDS

Adverbs may be preceded by the same signal words as adjectives. Pick out the signal words (intensifiers) in the following sentences and indicate whether the words they modify are adjectives or adverbs. (These signal words, or intensifiers, are often referred to as adverbs because they modify adjectives or adverbs.)

He played very well last night.
She looked quite beautiful in her new dress.
It was rather unfortunate that he had to leave.
He drives more carefully than I.

USING MODIFIERS EFFECTIVELY

Nouns and verbs provide the bone and muscle of our writing; they provide the essential framework. In order to flesh out the bones and muscles, to make our writing more colorful, vivid, and precise, we need modifiers. Consider, for instance, the following "skeleton" sentence:

The actress turned away from the crowd.

What information is communicated to us by the sentence? Is it sufficient? Does it create a vivid picture? Suppose we added two adjectives:

The *nervous* actress turned away from the *hostile* crowd.

The two adjectives bring the specific scene into a much sharper focus for us and help us to visualize what is happening. Suppose we changed the sentence to the following:

The *injured* actress turned away from the *astonished* crowd.

Now we have created a completely different scene from our "skeleton" sentence by simply changing the two adjectives. Each time you change the adjectives. you create a different scene for your reader. Try forming some different sentences of your own by changing the adjectives.

In the previous examples, the noun informed us *who* was performing the action (the "actress") and the verb told us *what* she did ("turned away"). To make the sentences more vivid and more exact, we needed adjectives ("nervous," "hostile," "injured," "astonished"). Suppose we had gone one step further and described *how* she performed the action. We could have written:

The nervous actress *quickly* turned away from the crowd.

If we had said that she turned "solemnly" or "slowly," we would have created a slightly different picture. We could have started our sentence with adverbs like "suddenly" or "then." If we wanted to qualify or limit the action of the actress, we could have used adverbs like "only," "merely" or "hardly."

Modifiers help us to add color, vitality, and precision to our writing by clarifying certain details and adding information about others. In order for adjectives and adverbs to be effective they must be vivid and precise, yet appropriate to the context of our writing.

VIVID ADJECTIVES

Return to our "skeleton" sentence for a moment. Suppose we wrote:

The *nice* actress turned away from the *big* crowd.

Does the addition of the adjectives "nice" and "big" add much more information or color to the sentence? Are these adjectives precise or vivid? They have been used so often to mean so many different things that they have lost any specific meaning they once had. We speak of a "big wedding," a "big jump in the cost of living," a "big down payment on a house," a "big piece of cake," a "big skyscraper," a "big insect." We talk about a "nice day," a "nice trip," a "nice girl," a "nice meal," a "nice figure," a "nice raise in pay." Effective adjectives should create pictures in our mind. Overworked adjectives like "nice" and "big" create only vague, general impressions. Avoid them. Develop the habit of taking time to search for "le mot juste," the carefully chosen word that has no frayed edges but conveys instantly the exact impression you want. If you are not satisfied with an adjective you have used, but cannot think of another, use your *Thesaurus*.

activities

1 In this activity you are going to test your own S.Q. (Synonym Quotient) by seeing how many suitable synonyms you can discover for our overworked adjective, "big." Without using a dictionary or *Thesaurus,* write a one-sentence description of each of the following. Use vivid adjectives, but make sure they are appropriate

for the nouns they modify. Try for as much variety as possible in your use of adjectives. When you have finished, compare your descriptions with those of the other class members.

crowd at a rock festival
moon rocket about to be launched
raise in pay
creature in a horror movie
wrestler
skyscraper
package of detergent
hotel ballroom
eyes
parade
army tank
slice of pie

2 a It's difficult to think of many synonyms for "big," isn't it? Perhaps S.Q.A.T. can help you. S.Q.A.T. is our Synonym Quotient Automatic Thesaurus computer. As you can see on this page, a student has fed the word "big" into the computer. If you turn to page 68, you will notice that S.Q.A.T. has provided him with a long list of synonyms. Try using some of them to improve the descriptions you wrote in activity 1. But be careful. If you use an adjective inappropriately simply because you think it sounds impressive (a "big" word), S.Q.A.T. will blow a fuse.

b Choose ten words from the S.Q.A.T. list in activity (a). Use each word in a sentence so that its meaning is clearly illustrated. Try to combine each adjective with an appropriate noun and create a vivid image.

67

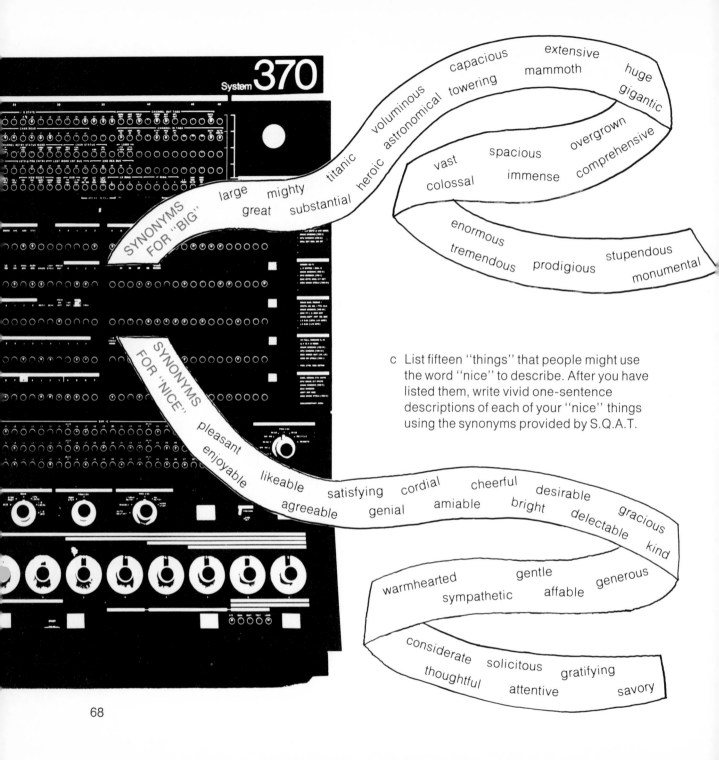

System **370**

SYNONYMS FOR "BIG"

large mighty
great substantial heroic titanic astronomical towering voluminous capacious mammoth extensive huge gigantic

vast spacious overgrown comprehensive
colossal immense
enormous stupendous
tremendous prodigious monumental

SYNONYMS FOR "NICE"

pleasant
enjoyable
likeable satisfying cordial cheerful desirable
agreeable genial amiable bright gracious
delectable kind

warmhearted gentle generous
sympathetic affable

considerate solicitous gratifying
thoughtful attentive savory

c List fifteen "things" that people might use
the word "nice" to describe. After you have
listed them, write vivid one-sentence
descriptions of each of your "nice" things
using the synonyms provided by S.Q.A.T.

d The following list contains examples of some other adjectives that have been weakened by overuse. Discuss each of these words in class and discover how many synonyms you can list for each of them. For each synonym you suggest you must also provide a suitable context in which it could be used. After you have finished your class discussion, consult a *Thesaurus* and add to your lists any suitable words you missed.

good	terrible
pretty	little
ugly	fast
great	slow
fine	funny
wonderful	fat
terrific	skinny
awful	beautiful

3 Write letters describing any of the items in activity 1. Write three letters, each written from the point of view of a different person. For instance, you might describe the crowd at a rock festival from the point of view of a singer performing there, a policeman in charge of crowd control, and a teen-ager attending his first rock festival. Specify to whom you are writing. The singer, for instance, might be writing to his manager, the policeman to his superior officer, and the teen-ager to his closest friend.

BEWARE OF ADJECTIVITIS!

For dinner I had an astronomical piece of pie and a prodigious scoop of ice cream.

The tired, weary, fatigued old pensioner plodded home.

The writers of the two sentences above are suffering from "adjectivitis," a disease of the mouth and pen. They have tried too hard to use vivid adjectives.

Once "adjectivitis" infects a healthy piece of writing it may prove fatal. The best precaution against contracting it is to make sure you know the meaning of each word you use and that you use it appropriately. The writer who used "astronomical" and "prodigious" to describe pie and ice cream misused these words in order to make his writing sound more learned or dignified. Don't be phony in your writing. If you are not comfortable with a word you have found in your *Thesaurus,* don't use it until you find out more about it.

The writer who overwhelmed the "pensioner" with four adjectives was also suffering from "adjectivitis." He piled on adjectives like logs on a fire. Be restrained in your use of adjectives. If a noun needs an adjective to clarify it or make it more vivid, then use an appropriate one. But if the noun is complete in itself, leave it alone.

BEWARE OF ADVERBITIS!

Healthy, active verbs can be crippled by unnecessary adverbs. The writer who suffers from adverbitis often demonstrates a lack of faith in the verbs he uses. He refuses to trust a verb like "return," for instance, and insists on writing sentences like the following:

He returned the overdue book back to the library. Yesterday Mr. Smith returned back home to Richmond.

He never feels that a verb is vivid enough by itself, but insists on trying to strengthen it by adding modifiers.

The President forcibly condemned the attack. The Yankees soundly trounced the Tigers.

The writer who suffers from adverbitis also has a compulsion to overuse words like "very," "quite," "rather." To him nothing is just important—it is *very* important; he is never just positive about something—he is *quite* positive; no room is ever quiet for him—it is *rather* quiet. He is also so *firmly* convinced about what he is doing that not only does he believe in it, but he *definitely* and *wholeheartedly* believes in it.

activity

Imagine that you are an editor for a large publisher. The following sentences are taken from a manuscript you have received from a writer who suffers from "adjectivitis" and "adverbitis." Strengthen his sentences by eliminating unnecessary adjectives and adverbs. Reword the sentences if necessary.

a It is an actual fact that the future prospects of modern young teen-agers of today are grim and not very hopeful. But, as is their usual custom, today's teens ignore the lessons of past history and live under false illusions that everything will work out to their advantage. Each and every teen should shake himself out of his apathy.

b Personally, it is my own opinion that woman is equally as good as man.

c The clever, bright, intelligent author gave me a free gift of his new book that has just been released. It is a popular best seller and has been read by thousands of people.

d As a rule, I am usually quite positive that what I do is absolutely right.

e His invention is a new innovation in the field of science. It provides both a sound audible to the ear and a signal visible to the eye.

f The real truth of the matter is that our tanks were surrounded on all sides by the enemy and our infantry had to retreat back to our lines. It was a very grave crisis.

SOME USAGE PROBLEMS WITH MODIFIERS

ALL RIGHT
The correct spelling is "all right." It should not be spelled any other way.

ALL READY, ALREADY
"All ready" means "completely prepared," "in a state of readiness." "Already" means "before or by the specified time."

The dancers were *all ready* to begin the performance.
The theatre was *already* full by curtain time.

ALL TOGETHER, ALTOGETHER
"All together" means "all in one place," "acting as a group." "Altogether" means "wholly," "entirely."

Our family was *all together* at last.
He was *altogether* unreasonable in his demands.

GOOD, WELL
"Good" is an adjective; "well" may be an adjective or an adverb. As an adjective, "well" means "in good health," "satisfactory."

We had a *good* time at the party. (adjective)
The cake tastes *good*.   (adjective)
Yesterday he wasn't very *well*.   (adjective meaning "in good health")
All is *well*. (adjective meaning "satisfactory")
He plays hockey *well*. (adverb modifying the verb "plays")

FEWER, LESS
"Fewer" refers to number, to the countable.

"Less" refers to amount or degree.

He spends *fewer* hours on his homework this year.
He spends *less* time on his homework this year.
He has *less* ability than his brother, but he makes *fewer* mistakes.

KIND OF, SORT OF
Use "kind of" and "sort of" rather than "kind of a" and "sort of a." See also page 34 for problems with expressions such as "these kind" or "those sort."'

What *kind of* (not: kind of a) book do you prefer?

ONLY
Limiting adverbs such as "only," "merely," "hardly," "nearly," "just" should be placed immediately before the words they modify.

He had a face *only* a mother could love. (not: He had only a face a mother could love.)
The bomb killed *only* one child. (not: The bomb only killed one child.)
The dress cost *almost* sixty dollars. (not: The dress almost cost sixty dollars.)

REAL, REALLY
In standard English, "real" is an adjective meaning "genuine." It is sometimes used in informal spoken English as an adverb meaning "very," "extremely." In written English, however, "really" is the accepted adverb to mean "very," "extremely," or "actually."

Is that painting *real*? (meaning "genuine")
He was *really* (very, extremely) tired last night. (preferable to "He was real tired last night.")

STRUCTURE WORDS— PRONOUNS, CONJUNCTIONS, PREPOSITIONS

Ask half the class to list all the nouns in English. Ask the other half to list all the pronouns (I, you . . .) in English. Why would the first half object to this task?

This little example assignment illustrates one of the important differences between *form class words* and *structure words.* Each of the three main classes of structure words (pronouns, conjunctions, prepositions) consists of a relatively small set of words. On the other hand, each of the four main form classes (nouns, verbs, adjectives, adverbs) is very large—so large that not even a dictionary is able to include them all. Take all the form class words out of a dictionary and you would be left with probably less than several hundred words. Take all the structure words out of a dictionary and probably no one would notice.

If so, why bother about structure words at all? How can it be that in any sample of speech or writing the most frequently repeated words are usually structure words?

Obviously, nouns, verbs, adjectives, and adverbs are the principal items that carry meaning in a sentence. Any message depends very largely for its content on form class words. Consider this example:

Happy boy jumped narrow stream.

While the message may sound telegraphic, the situation is relatively clear in meaning; the event, the characters, the scene, the setting are all present and understood. The elements of the mental picture are all there.

What the "sentence picture" needs, however, is some sort of electric circuitry which will supply the current to get the picture moving. Structure words provide the wiring circuits that allow the message to spring to life. Does the boy jump "over," "into," or "out of" the narrow stream? Is it "a" boy or "the" stream?

Just as many different messages may be run over the same single electric circuit, so too, many different form class words may operate with just a few structure words. Let us complete the example sentence by supplying the "juice" of structure words:

The happy boy jumped *over a* narrow stream.

If you substitute other form class words for these, the possible number of different sentences that might be formed would be enormous. A small number of structure words allows a tremendous number of messages to flow.

The_____ _____ _____over a_____
_____.

An electric current will flow if certain connections are made. Once the connections are made, the direction of the flow can be altered. And this is principally what structure words do; they operate as connectors, or as directors. They can shut the current of the message on and off, and they can direct the path of its flow. Here are some examples.

Structure words are:

1 *connectors* (or, and, but, who, which . . .)
2 *directors*   (into, out of, over, under, beside, with . . .)

PRONOUNS

Pronouns can be categorized as either form class words or as structure words, depending on their type and function. The *personal pronouns* (I, me, you, he, him, she, her, it, we, they, them) are actually form class words because they inflect. Moreover, the personal pronoun, as its name tells us, shares all the meaning and force of the noun for which it stands.
The personal pronouns act merely as a sort of abbreviation for a previously stated noun.
We know, for instance, that the symbol IBM is merely a shortened form that stands for the complete name, International Business Machines. The personal pronouns do exactly the same thing, as is shown in this example:

Mr. Brown phoned the police. *He* was . . .

And so if nouns are form class words, then those personal pronouns which stand for nouns must also be considered form class words. The personal pronouns merely form a sub-class of the larger class of words which we call nouns.

There are other types of pronouns, however, which seem to work in quite a different way. Consider these examples:

Relative pronouns:

The man *who* came to dinner . . .
The cow *that* jumped over the moon . . .
The question *which* I asked . . .

These pronouns act as connectors; they tie whole clauses or sentences into other clauses or sentences. Since connectors are structure words, then relative pronouns are clearly different from the personal pronouns. Their function of standing for a noun seems to be less important than their connecting function.

Consider, as well, these other types of pronouns:

Demonstrative pronouns:

This is mine.
That sounds wrong.

Interrogative pronouns:

Which do you want?
What did I tell you?
Who went into the store?

Again, these pronouns do more than simply stand for other nouns. They ask questions; they point out other words for attention. They direct our attention to other parts of a sentence.

Like connectors, directors are classified as structure words. As you look back over the examples, it is easy to see that relative, demonstrative, and interrogative pronouns are more important for the work they do as connectors and directors than merely as symbols for nouns.

CONJUNCTIONS

As the word *conjunction* implies (it literally means "with a joining"), the function of such words is to connect. Conjunctions may connect two (or more) words, phrases, clauses, or sentences, as in these examples:

bread *and* honey
The boy gave the money to his sister *and* to his brother.
Joan sings very well, but she does not want to be in the show.

There is, however, a difference in the way any two sets of words may be connected. When two word groups are joined, each group may be independent enough to stand alone without the connection if it had to. An equal joining of this nature is referred to as "co-ordination."

In another type of joining, one word group is dependent upon the other for its completeness. This dependent or subordinate word group could not stand alone if the independent word group were taken away. That kind of relationship is called "subordination."

Different types of conjunctions are used to make connections between groups that are both independent and between groups in which one is subordinated to the other. *Co-ordinating conjunctions* connect independent groups of words. *Subordinating conjunctions* join a dependent group of words to an independent group.

Co-ordinating conjunctions:

and, but, or, yet, . . .

Subordinating conjunctions:

when, where, while, that, because, if, until, unless, . . .

Study the way in which these two sentences are connected. Which involves co-ordination, and which involves subordination?

Mary saw the cake, and she immediately wanted to eat it.
When Mary saw the cake, she immediately wanted to eat it.

In each of the examples, are the two combining sentences able to stand alone when connected? What is the difference between the independent structure of "Mary saw the cake" and the sub-ordinated structure of "When Mary saw the cake"?

PREPOSITIONS

When first learning to speak in sentences, very young children frequently fail to use structure words. A child's grammar is almost entirely a language of form class words. Consider, for instance, this possible exchange between a mother and her child.

Child: Daddy shoe.
Mother: Yes, give the shoe *to* daddy.
   or
       Daddy's shoe is *under* the table.
   or
       Don't hit daddy *with* the shoe.

Notice what the parent is doing. She takes the scant statement of the child and expands or elaborates on it. Reading from the clues provided by the situation, the mother elaborates on the child's telegraphic speech. Much of the time, the process of elaboration requires the parent to supply the missing *prepositions*— words which explain the position, space, and time relationships in the real world. Study this partial list of prepositions:

above, on   up, down
before, after   along, with
beside, behind, between   over, under

By supplying such words, parents are not so much correcting the child's faulty grammar as they are helping the child to understand the world around him—a world where objects appear "above," "below," "beside," or "behind" other objects; a world where events occur "before" or "after" other events. By "directing" the child's thought processes, parents are helping in the natural development of mental thought. Prepositions are directors; that is to say, they are structure words.

Try describing the physical or positional relationships between different objects in a room, say, your classroom, or your kitchen. Notice what you are forced to do. First, you must name the objects themselves: books, chairs, desks, windows, and so on. To do this you must use nouns. Second, to direct your listener's attention correctly, you must explain the physical relationship between these various objects. To do this, you must use prepositions such as "beside," "across," "behind," and so on. Prepositions, therefore, always work along with nouns (or pronouns). Such a grouping is called a *prepositional phrase.* Study these examples:

with my books
beside the counter
across the aisle
over the moon
under the water
against him

How can you tell from these examples that nouns (or pronouns) following prepositions are always objects of the preposition? Don't forget that a noun can be the object of a preposition as well as the object of a verb. As you will see later in the book, words in a sentence fall into natural groups, and one of these natural groupings is the prepositional phrase.

ADSPEAK
THE GRAMMAR
OF ADVERTISING

ADSPEAK—THE GRAMMAR OF ADVERTISING

Have you ever read an ad in a newspaper or magazine or seen a commercial on TV and felt that it was written just for you, that the product advertised was exactly what you needed or wanted? The people who design ads hope you will respond in this manner. To achieve this result, they use a variety of resources to appeal to the potential buyers (the audience) of their product: color, photos, design, layout, different kinds of print, and so on. They also use language.

WHAT IS ADSPEAK?

Our purpose in this chapter is to examine the language (the "copy") of print advertising, the kind you normally find in newspapers and magazines. Studies have shown that the grammar of advertising copy differs from the grammar normally used in other kinds of writing. The ad on page 79 indicates to you some of these differences.

When the copywriter is writing an ad, he obviously does not say to himself, "By gosh, I think I'll use a concrete noun and three compound adjectives here." On the other hand, he is not free to use language any way he likes. He must be certain that the language he uses is appropriate for the specific audience he has in mind. He uses all his verbal skills to convince a specific audience to buy a specific product. In the following pages we investigate some of these language skills, and in the process discover how the copywriter uses grammar for his own purposes.

1 In each of the ads in this chapter you are going to try to sum up the specific point the copywriter is trying to make about his product. For the sake of convenience, we refer to it as the "message" of the ad. What is the message of the Clairol ad on page 79?

2 List the key words and note what part of speech each word is.

3 How does the picture in the ad reinforce the message conveyed by the copy?

4 Count the number of words in the ad. (Ignore the words on the bottle.) List the words in columns under the following headings: NOUNS, ADJECTIVES, VERBS, ADVERBS. Once you have listed and counted these words, it will be obvious which two parts of speech occur most often. How important are they to this ad?

5 Examine the nouns used. Which kind do you find more of—concrete or abstract? Why does the copywriter rely on this kind of noun?

6 Examine the adjectives used. Separate your list into two categories: those which give specific, concrete information ("green"), and those which simply give a general but attractive description ("breathtaking"). Which type predominates in most advertising? Why?

7 Examine the verbs. Contrast the copywriter's use of verbs with his use of nouns and adjectives. Which is the key verb in the ad? Why does the copywriter use this verb rather than the one normally used in ads—the verb "try," as in, "Try it, you'll like it"?

8 For what specific audience is this ad designed? Show how the copywriter has used language to appeal to this audience. Would this ad appeal to a group of boys? Why, or why not?

9 In the following pages, there are several ads for class discussion. In addition, you will receive "memos" from the Nelson, Nelson, & Nelson, Inc. advertising agency. Imagine that the members of your class are copywriters in this agency. The class may be divided into groups according to the instructions of your teacher. The task of each group is to write copy for an ad designed to sell the product mentioned in the memo. You do not have to draw the visual part of the ad, but you should describe it in an accompanying paragraph. Each group should submit its "ad" to the rest of the class for reactions to it. (The memo containing your first assignment is on page 82.)

Inside this bottle are the most breathtaking green smells on this earth, in a shampoo so exciting it does beautiful things to the inside of your head, too.

Experience it.

Clairol* herbal essence shampoo with protein from natural sources and the enchanted essences of 19 mysterious green herbs and tiny wildflowers. It makes your hair crystal clean and shining and very, very excited. And fresh as the first day of spring in a garden of Earthly Delights*.

In two formulas for normal-to-dry or oily hair.

A LUXURIOUS DYED LILAC FULLY LET OUT PRIME MINK FLOOR LENGTH COAT
WITH A DYED MATCHING FOX COLLAR AND DETACHABLE BORDER THAT CAN BECOME
A MAGNIFICENT STRAIGHT STOLE. DESIGNED AND CREATED EXCLUSIVELY BY US.
FOR FINE EXCLUSIVE FURS AT SENSIBLE PRICES VISIT OUR FUR SALONS.

FURS *by Mannis*

| 104 South Beverly Drive | CAESARS PALACE HOTEL | INTERNATIONAL HOTEL | 352 Seventh Avenue |
| Beverly Hills, California 90212 | Las Vegas, Nevada 89109 | Las Vegas, Nevada 89109 | New York, New York 10001 |

1 What is the message of the Mannis Fur ad on the opposite page? What are the key words in the copy of the ad? How does the picture reinforce the copy?

2 List the nouns, adjectives, verbs, and adverbs used in the copy. Which part of speech occurs most often? Why should this part of speech be emphasized in an ad of this kind?

3 Examine the adjectives used. Separate them into two lists as you did with the Clairol ad — those which give specific, concrete information and those which simply give a general but attractive description. Which kind predominates here? Why does the copywriter stress this kind?

4 Examine the list of nouns. What do the nouns used have in common? Why are there more than twice as many adjectives as nouns in this ad?

5 How many verbs are used? How many adverbs? Which adverb is simply the adverbial form of an adjective used in the copy? Why has the copywriter emphasized this word by a subtle kind of repetition?

6 How has the copywriter used language to appeal to the specific audience for whom this ad is designed?

nelson nelson & nelson

FROM: J. Handlebuck

TO: All copywriters

RE: Cleano Cosmetics account

Cleano Cosmetics has asked us to design two ads: one
for a new men's shampoo and the other for a new men's
hair spray. They have requested us to suggest names
for each of these products and design suitable ads to
be placed in various magazines for men. There is no
need for me to stress to you how important this account
is to our company. I expect to see some creative ads
that will win the Cleano Cosmetics account for us!

J.C.F. Handlebuck,
Vice-President
JCFH:ad

1 What is the "message" of the Parfums Rochas ad on this page?

2 How is the language of this ad suitable for its audience?

3 Make noun, adjective, verb, and adverb lists as you did for the previous ads. Note which part of speech predominates.

4 Comment on the effectiveness of the nouns used in the Parfums Rochas ad. Which three nouns are used at least four times each in this ad? When you first read the ad, did you notice this repetition? Explain why the copywriter has repeated these nouns.

5 Contrast the Parfums Rochas ad with the Clairol ad on page 79. How do they differ in tone? According to the ads, what is the purpose of each product? Comment on the sentence structure in the two ads. How is the sentence structure of each ad appropriate for the specific audience of that ad?

"It's time someone told you the truth about perfume. It might as well be me."

The truth about perfume is remarkably simple: There is no fragrance that will transform a woman into something she isn't. But a fragrance can do something terribly important. It can suggest the woman you are within.

Audace is my newest fragrance. You might consider it part of your passport to the new freedom. For it enables the new woman to make her own bold statement, the one that has always been there, but has waited until now to be expressed.

Another of my fragrances, for perhaps another mood, is Femme. Infinitely feminine, this perfume enhances the serenity of the wearer. Femme is, after all, just another way of saying: Woman.

And then there is Madame Rochas. A fragrance that suggests everything, but surrenders nothing.

So choose wisely and never ask more of your perfume than you ask of yourself.

Rochas Paris creates Audace, Femme, Madame Rochas. For men, Monsieur Rochas and Moustache.

PARFUMS ROCHAS

nelson nelson & nelson

FROM: J. Handlebuck
TO: All copywriters
RE: Parfums Rochas account

I am requesting your suggestions for two new ads:

1. The "Parfums Rochas" people have asked us to design an ad for their new men's cologne called "Monsieur Rochas." They stipulate that this ad must be similar in tone to their "Parfums Rochas" ad. They also want us, as much as possible, to imitate the same kind of sentence structure, emphasize the same parts of speech, and use the same device of "subtle" repetition.

2. They also want us to design an ad for their new men's After Shave and suggest a name for it. This product is intended for the rugged, virile, outdoor type of man. They have tentatively named it "HE-MAN," but hope that we can come up with a much better name for their product.

May I remind all of you that, unless we come up with some spectacular ads, our payroll list will be much shorter next month.

J.C.F. Handlebuck,
Vice-President
JCFH:ad

84

THERE IS ANOTHER TIME, ANOTHER PLACE.

You're standing on seven miles of sand looking straight west to Japan.

Last week you felt the warmth of a bonfire in our Cariboo country, tasted fresh fruit from our orchards, touched cedar trees that were fifteen feet around in a park in the middle of a metropolis.

You've seen a quiet island city that appeared to have been plucked from the pages of Charles Dickens, and you've heard the cry of eagles over a misty rainforest.

You've gone as far as you can go on the west coast of Canada. And in the process of losing the world, you've found yourself.

THE TIME IS FALL.
THE PLACE IS BRITISH COLUMBIA.

1. What type of audience is the British Columbia ad on page 84 appealing to? How is the tone of the ad appropriate for both the audience and the product?

2. List the parts of speech as you have done for the previous ads in this chapter. What part of speech is emphasized the most? Why is this emphasis appropriate for this ad?

3. Note the nouns used. What picture of British Columbia do you see in your imagination as you read down the list of nouns? Is it what the copywriter wanted you to visualize?

4. Note the verbs used. There are more here than we usually find in ads, but the copywriter has used them for a specific purpose. What is his purpose?

5. Note the adjectives used. Do they add specific information, or do they simply give a general but attractive description? How do they differ from the adjectives generally used in the ads you have studied so far? Why has the copywriter used this kind of adjective?

6. There aren't many adverbs used. Have there been many used in any of the ads we have studied so far? How do you account for the lack of adverbs?

7. Write the copy for an ad inviting people to visit your state at a specific season or time of the year.

8. Using words from the British Columbia ad, or from the ad you have written about your own state, write a poem describing that state.

Examine the following three automobile ads.

Is nothing sacred?

Here we've been slaving away for 25 years, improving the Volkswagen's insides, and letting the outside take care of itself.

And now—boom! People are trying to show us how it ought to be done.

"Why?" we asked.

"To make it look as good as it really is."

O.K. Maybe they've got a point. The VW is an amazingly advanced car.

The engine is a precision masterpiece, carved out of aluminum-magnesium alloy.

It sits in back, over the drive wheels. The traction is unbelievable.

The engine is cooled by air. You simply never think about water or antifreeze.

Oil? Hardly any ever. Gas? About 26 miles per gallon of regular.

The Volkswagen's suspension is like a sports car's, its finish like a limousine's.

Almost anywhere you go in the world, a VW has been before.

Its funny shape has become the international symbol of quality and reliability.

"Never change it," people beg us. And now we beg the same of you.

Wanted: Men who can handle a real road machine. Dodge Challenger Rallye.

There are special men who develop an almost spiritual attachment to their cars. They want a no-nonsense road machine that grabs a rough, winding stretch of road and holds on. One that stays low and close to the road like a snake. For these men, Dodge builds Challenger Rallye. A trim, taut, tough car that hugs every inch of road it goes over. Why?

Because of Challenger's torsion bar suspension. No mushy coil springs for this car—only responsive torsion bars and leaf springs will do. They combine to give you a firm, honest ride all the time.

These special men will also appreciate Challenger's Electronic Ignition System. Because there are no points and condenser, this system is virtually mainte-

nance free and your tuneup costs will be reduced. Neither wet nor weather affect this special system. And each spark plug will get up to 35 percent more starting voltage every time.

Dodge Challenger Rallye. A special kind of road machine for a special breed of men. Test-drive one at your nearby Dodge Dealer's today.

Extra care in engineering makes a difference in Dodge...depend on it.

Jaguar V-12.
New breed of power.

Smooth, silken power.

That is the inherent nature of the Jaguar V-12.

It is a powerplant so logically designed, so perfectly balanced that it sets new standards in engine performance.

The twelve pistons exert such a constantly even force on the crankshaft that the result approaches turbine-like smoothness.

For example, while 0 to 60 in 6.8 seconds is impressive, it's not nearly as impressive as the feeling of smoothness and steadiness with which that performance is achieved.

Impressive also, is the available reservoir of torque. In any gear, at virtually any driving speed, our V-12 gives you instant power to pass, to avoid, to leave congestion in the rear-view mirror.

In fact, at 10 mph in *top* gear you can skim up the scale to cruising speed without so much as a shudder.

This performance comes directly from our basic design. Instead of a temperamental racing engine, we developed an engine that thrives in *your* driving world—docile at the stop light, polite in traffic, yet incredibly able outside the 30-mile limit.

So, in addition to its smoothness and 5.3 litres of power, our V-12 has—

Single overhead cams for simplicity. Aluminum-alloy block, heads and sump for lightness. Flat-faced heads for excellent torque in the lower- and middle-range speeds. And instead of a conventional ignition system, we have a transistorized one that obviates the need for points.

This new breed of power is set into the classic breed of cat—the Jaguar E-type 2 + 2 and convertible.

It's a suitable setting, indeed. Power-assisted all-around disc brakes. Power-assisted rack and pinion steering. Independent rear suspension. "Anti-dive" front suspen-

sion. Four-speed synchromesh manual transmission (a through-the-gears automatic is optional).

Plus all the luxury, comfort and instrumentation that you would expect in a Jaguar cockpit.

So before you judge the power of any other sports car, get a taste of the new breed: Jaguar V-12. At your Jaguar dealer.

For his name and for information about overseas delivery, call (800) 447-4700. In Illinois, call (800) 322-4400. Calls are toll free.

BRITISH LEYLAND MOTORS INC., LEONIA, N. J. 07605

Jaguar

1 For what specific audience is each of the automobile ads designed?

2 Show how the language used in the Jaguar ad is appropriate for the audience. List an adjective, a noun, and a verb from this ad which would be totally inappropriate for a Volkswagen ad.

3 Select a person in the class to explain the technical detail in the Jaguar ad to the rest of the class.

4 Show how the language used in the Volkswagen ad contrasts with that of the Jaguar ad. Consider such factors as the kind of words used, the length and type of sentences, and the general tone. Quote four words used in the Volkswagen ad that would never appear in a Jaguar ad. How does the picture in the Volkswagen ad increase its effectiveness? Contrast it with the picture in the Jaguar ad.

5 List five adjectives used in the Dodge Challenger ad which would appeal to its audience. What other words or phrases are used specifically for this audience? How does the picture in the ad increase its effectiveness? Would the tone and language of this ad be appropriate for a Jaguar ad? for a Volkswagen ad? Why, or why not?

nelson nelson & nelson

FROM: J. Handlebuck

TO: All copywriters

RE: Jaguar, Dodge,
       Volkswagen accounts

We have received some unusual requests from our three major automobile accounts. They want:

1. A Jaguar ad designed to appeal to very rich women who are not interested in engineering data or performance statistics.
2. A Dodge Challenger ad designed to appeal to a young, swinging crowd.
3. A Volkswagen ad designed to appeal to wealthy business men.

Because of our recent loss of two major accounts, it is imperative that we all pull together to produce some exciting new ads!

J.C.F. Handlebuck,
Vice-President.

JCFH:ad

Women don't travel like they used to.

Used to be a lady only tagged along. But not today.

Today's woman goes far on her own merits, thank you.

And when she does travel with a friend, it's United Air Lines.

Not just because United's a place-to-place airline with more places to offer than anyone else in your land.

But because we're a people-to-people airline.

People who take your bags at curbside and wish you welcome. People who'll find the right gate. The right meal. And the right way to get you there.

You know, the only limits today are in a lady's head.

So when you're ready to take off and fly, call your Travel Agent or United. You'll find a friend in the friendly skies.

The friendly skies of your land.
United Air Lines
Partners in Travel with Western International Hotels.

He didn't want to spoil his mother's Thanksgiving dinner by being late.

This Thanksgiving, don't drive as though your dinner depended on it.
Drive as though your life depended on it.

Mobil
We want you to live.

1 What is the message of the United Air Lines ad on page 89? For whom is the ad designed? Examine the sentences used in this ad and note which are complete sentences and which are fragments. Why does the copywriter use so many fragments?

2 ''Women don't travel like they used to.'' Why would some grammarians object to this statement? Why did the copywriter word it this way? What other famous ad makes the same ''mistake''? How have the advertisers built an entire advertising campaign around this ''mistake''? What other ads use ''mistakes'' in grammar?

3 Which nouns are used more than once in this ad? Why? How does the copywriter form adjectives from some of these nouns?

4 What does the picture contribute to this ad?

5 Which is more important in the Mobil ad on this page—the picture or the copy? Why isn't there more copy? The copywriter uses the phrase ''as though'' twice in this ad. He could have used the preposition ''like,'' which was used in the United Air Lines ad. This usage would also be considered incorrect by some people. Why did he choose to use ''as though'' rather than ''like''?

6 How is the language used in the Brunswick ad on page 91 appropriate for the picture? Give specific examples. Which is the key noun used? This is the noun around which the whole ad is constructed. Which other nouns support the general message? Which adjectives?

7 Why is this ad so effective?

There's a little bit of hustler in all of us.

Now we think pool is the grandest game in the world.

And heaven knows, there are few greater pleasures than having a pool table of your own.

But you might as well know one thing right now.

You can't trust anyone with a pool cue in his hands.

You can take the sweetest, kindest, gentlest souls on earth and invite them over for a friendly game.

And the next thing you know you've got your sleeves rolled up and your earnest money down, fighting for your life in a game of Eight-Ball or Straight Pool.

Oh, some people will tell you pool is a gentleman's game.

But don't you believe it.

We've been making pool tables since 1845.

And there's a little bit of hustler in all of us.

Brunswick
Consumer Division Brunswick Corporation

The Matador. One of the new Brunswick slate tables for 1971.
Others available in every price range.

nelson nelson & nelson

FROM: J. Handlebuck

TO: All copywriters

RE: Brunswick account

We have received instructions to prepare two ads for Brunswick pool tables. The first ad is to be designed to appeal to young executives on the way up. The second is to appeal to the wives of these men.

May I make one final plea for excellence to all copywriters employed by the company. Our track record so far has been dismal. I beg you to use all your creativity to design innovative and exciting ads. PLEASE!!

J. Handlebuck

1 The billboard ad below was very popular and won a place in the advertising industry's best ads yearbook. Give reasons why you think it deserved or did not deserve such acclaim.

2 The Volkswagen company also ran a magazine ad using the same picture and caption, but including copy. That ad won a Gold Medal Award from the advertising industry. Try writing your own copy for this ad. When you are finished, turn the page and compare yours with the original.

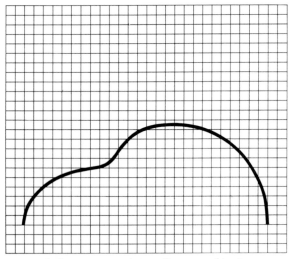

Is the economy trying to tell you something?

Volkswagen Canada Ltd.

ADSPEAK RESEARCH

After analyzing the grammar of the ads presented in this book, you can probably make certain generalizations about the grammar of advertising. However, any selection of ads presented in a book is necessarily limited. If you want a valid study of the language of advertising, you must collect many examples of various kinds of ads for your analysis. A study of this kind was conducted in England by Geoffrey Leech and the results published in his book, *English in Advertising*. You might be interested in taking some of his findings and investigating advertising in the United States to see if his results hold true here also.

SOME CHARACTERISTICS OF ADSPEAK

1 Advertising vocabulary is colloquial, not formal.

2 Imperatives are very frequent in advertising English.

3 The majority of nouns in advertising copy are concrete and refer directly to the product.

4 Words like "thirst-quenching" and "taste-tempting" are instances of a hallmark of advertising English: the adjective compound.

5 Advertising language is marked by a wealth of adjective vocabulary and a poverty of verb vocabulary.

6 The suffix "y"—as in chunky, chewy, creamy, crispy, crunchy, juicy, meaty, nutty, silky, spicy—is by far the most frequent adjective suffix in advertising copy.

7 "Good" and "new" are more than twice as popular as any other adjective in advertising copy.

8 Advertising English frequently uses unqualified comparatives. For instance, an ad may state that a certain product "makes your clothes whiter" without ever stating "whiter" than what. No standard of comparison is given.

activity

Divide the class into groups. Each group is responsible for collecting and analyzing ads from magazines and newspapers over a period of time stipulated by your teacher. Your group should choose a certain category of ads for its study: women's cosmetics, food products, automobiles, clothing, men's cosmetics, toys, furniture, appliances, or any other product.

a The form of your analysis should be decided by the class in general. You may want to use the approach used with the ads in this chapter; you may want to use the characteristics of Adspeak; or you may develop criteria of your own. After completing your analysis, write it in the form of a report and present it to the rest of the class. Please make sure, however, that you stress the *grammar* of advertising in your report.

b In a study of newspaper ads for women's clothing, the most commonly used adjectives (in order) were the following:

1 new	11 high
2 good	12 perfect
3 soft	13 smooth
4 warm	14 luxurious
5 free	15 slim
6 full	16 smart
7 lovely	17 fashionable
8 wonderful	18 practical
9 easy	19 washable
10 light	

In your report in (a), include a frequency list like the one above for the most commonly used adjectives in your group's category.

c In a study of television commercials, the 20 most commonly used verbs (in order) were the following:

1 make	11 look
2 get	12 need
3 give	13 love
4 have	14 use
5 see	15 feel
6 buy	16 like
7 come	17 choose
8 go	18 take
9 know	19 start
10 keep	20 taste

In your report in (a), include a frequency list like the one above for the most commonly used verbs in your group's category. If possible, have your reports duplicated for the other members of your class.

Why a boy gives a girl flowers.

He said he gave me flowers because flowers are soft and pretty.

He said he gave me flowers because they're something real and honest.

He said he gave me flowers because those are the things I am.

And I hope he's right, because that's what I try to be.

Everything natural, the

way nature is.

Even with the perfume I wear.

Muguet des bois. Which means "Flower of the Woods." And that's as natural as you can get.

Something soft and pretty, real and honest.

Muguet des bois by Coty

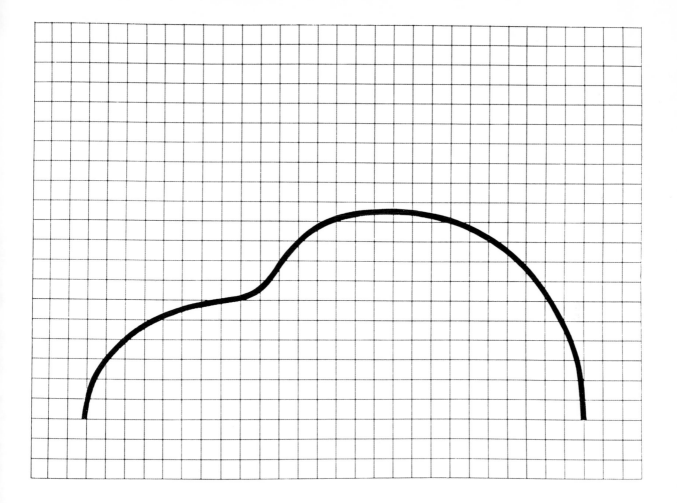

Is the economy trying to tell you something?

If you've hesitated about buying a new car because of the economy, maybe you should look into the economy of buying a new Volkswagen.

To begin with, while the average new car sells for about $3185, a new VW sells for only $1839*.

That saves you about $1300.

Then, while the average car costs 10.9 cents a mile to run, a Volkswagen costs only 5 cents.

That saves you about another $700

every year (or 12,000 miles) you drive

And in just one year, it can bring your total savings to $2000.

In two years, $2700.

In three, $3400.

Happy days are here again.

COMMON
USAGE
PROBLEMS

Winstons taste good like a cigarette should.

(Sara Lee. . .) Nobody doesn't like Sara Lee.

VOICE OF THE PEOPLE

Us Tareyton smokers would rather fight than switch!

Everyone has their own special reasons for BankAmericard.

Schweppervescence

Bad grammar in ads directed at children

Wometco Ltd. (owned by Coca-Cola) has just started advertising a new soft drink called Mr. PiBB with the slogan "a real easy taste that goes down good."

In that one phrase I count two intentional grammatical errors and two intentional incorrect word usages.

I always thought that the Winston cigarette ads were the low-water mark in incomprehensible English grammar, but Mr. PiBB has them beat hands down. Perhaps Winston can be excused because their ads are directed at adults who presumably recognize the intentional grammatical errors. However, Mr. PiBB cannot be so excused as its ads are directed at children. If children are subjected to intentional bad grammar, and if they are given no way of even guessing that it is indeed intentional bad grammar, how can we expect children to learn proper grammar?

I realize the parent Coca-Cola company has probably spent thousands of dollars developing the advertising campaign to give Mr. PiBB a "just folks" image. But I believe that the advertising will probably do Coca-Cola more harm than good in Vancouver. . .

Perhaps we should ask the Coca-Cola company to withdraw its advertisements or to label them with the words "this advertisement contains incorrect grammar."

Roedy Green
Vancouver

THE ORANGE MOSTEST DRINK IN THE WHOLE WORLD.

When you're running like there's no tomorrow—Valvoline

A REAL EASY TASTE THAT GOES DOWN GOOD!

Mrs. Hamilton's 16-year old Maytag keeps working like it was born yesterday.

COMMON USAGE PROBLEMS

ACCEPT, EXCEPT—see page 57.

ADVICE, ADVISE—see page 34.

AIN'T
Although "ain't" has been used by a great many respected and educated authors in the past, it is a word with a bad reputation today. There are so many people who brand the use of this word as "uneducated," "ignorant," or "stupid" that it is wise to avoid using it. Certain uses of it, however, although considered nonstandard, are *not* illogical. Consider how we form contractions for the verb "to be":

He is not = He isn't (Isn't he?)
You are not = You aren't (Aren't you?)
I am not =   ?   (?)

How do we form the contraction for "I am not"? Following the same process,

I am not = I amn't (Amn't I?)

"Amn't" was the logical form. It was difficult to pronounce, however, and over the years people started to substitute "ain't," which was more easily said. ("Amn't" is still used in certain English dialects.) Gradually, however, "ain't" began to be condemned by educated speakers and writers and came to be considered "uneducated" usage. Some day it may again be widely accepted, especially as a useful contraction for "Am I not?" But because of the social and educational pressures against its use today, it should be avoided in both formal and informal writing and speaking.

Rather than using "Ain't I?", most people today use the form "Aren't I?" and consider it perfectly correct. Is this form any more grammatical than "Ain't I?"

ALL RIGHT—see page 71.

ALL READY, ALREADY—see page 71.

ALL TOGETHER, ALTOGETHER—see page 71.

ANYWAY, ANYWHERE, NOWHERE
A final "s" should not be used; the words are "anyway," "anywhere," "nowhere."

I don't feel like talking *anyway*. (not: anyways)
The dog may be hiding *anywhere*. (not: anywheres)
The silly dog is *nowhere* to be found. (not: nowheres)

AS WELL AS
In abbreviated expressions of comparison, do not drop the second "as."

He sings *as well as*, if not better than, I. (not: as well, if not better than)
Tangerines are *as good as*, if not better than, oranges. (not: as good, if not better than)

BESIDE, BESIDES
"Besides" means "placed or located at the side of something," whereas "besides" means "in addition to."

There were two very angry parents sitting *beside* us at the meeting.
There were many other angry parents at the meeting *besides* us.

BETWEEN, AMONG
"Between" refers to two persons or things, while "among" refers to more than two.

Between the two of us we will solve the problem. He didn't want to divide his money *among* all his greedy relatives.

BRING, TAKE—see page 57.

COMMA SPLICE— see page 142.

DANGLING MODIFIERS—see page 148.

DONE—see page 57.

DON'T—see page 57.

DOUBLE NEGATIVE
1 Following a negative in the verb, the words "some" or "something" become "any" or "anything," but not "no" or "nothing."

I have some money. I *don't* have *any* money. (not: no money)
I still have something left. I *don't* have *anything* left. (not: nothing left)

2 The words "hardly" and "scarcely" have the force of negatives and therefore must be followed by "any" or "anything."

I hardly have *any* money left. (not: no money)
I scarcely have *anything* left. (not: nothing left)

3 Unlike many other European languages, the negative in a simple English sentence must be attached either to the verb or to other words like "nowhere," "no one," "nothing"; the

negative should not appear in both positions.

I *didn't* go anywhere that evening with anyone, I went *nowhere* that evening with *no one*.

4 Two negatives in a sentence may sometimes have the force of an affirmative or probably affirmative statement.

I *didn't* say that I *don't* agree. (I may agree.)
I *don't* want you to think that you are *not* guilty. (You are guilty.)

EFFECT, AFFECT—see page 36.

EVERYBODY, EVERYONE
These pronouns, as well as similar indefinite pronouns, are usually considered singular by grammarians. In most cases they are followed by the singular form of the verb:

Everyone *loves* a winner. (not: Everyone love a winner.)

Everybody *is* here today. (not: Everybody are here today.)

There is a problem, however, when these words are used in sentences containing other pronouns which refer back to "everybody" or "everyone." If "everyone" and "everybody" are singular, then according to the "rule" any other words referring to them must be singular also.

Everyone must bring *his* lunch tomorrow. (not: their lunches)
The teacher told everyone to take *his* books home. (not: their books)

But consider sentences like the following. Do the sentences make sense if you use the singular forms, "he" and "his"?

Although yesterday I told everyone to bring (his, their) books to class, (he, they) forgot to do so. Everyone was waiting for me at the station, and (he, they) applauded loudly when I arrived.

It seems that there are occasions when the plural forms must be used. Words like "everybody" and "everyone," although singular in form, are often plural in meaning: they can mean "all people." Consequently, it is impossible to consider them singular in all cases. When they are obviously plural, use a plural pronoun.

FEWER, LESS—see page 71.

GOOD, WELL—see page 71.

HANGED, HUNG—see page 57.

I, ME
"I" is used when it is the subject of a verb; "me" is used when it is the object of a verb or preposition.

1 "Between you and me," not "between you and I," because the pronoun is the object of the preposition "between."

2 Use "he and I" as a subject of a sentence, not "him and me."

   He and I are great friends. (not: him and me)

3 In response to a question such as "Who is at the door?" you may say either "It's me" or "It is I," depending on whether you want to sound informal or pedantic. It would depend on whose doorbell you were ringing.

IMPLY, INFER—see page 57.

IN REGARD TO
The expression is "in regard to" or "regarding," but not "in regards to."

The President was uncertain about what action he should take *in regard to* (or *regarding*) the release of the White House tapes. (but not: in regards to)

IS (WHEN), IS (WHERE), IS (BECAUSE)
When defining or explaining, avoid the "is when," "is where," "is because" structure to introduce noun clauses.

A soliloquy is a speech given by an actor alone on stage. (not: A soliloquy is when an actor speaks alone on stage.)

The climax of the play may be defined as the point of greatest impact. (not: The climax is where the play achieves its greatest impact.)

The reason I came back is that I could not leave without you. (not: The reason I came back is because I could not leave without you.)

IT'S, ITS
"It's" is the contraction for "it is"; "its" is the possessive adjective.

The hurricane reached *its* full force about midnight. *It's* a hurricane, all right!

KIND OF, SORT OF—see page 71.

KIND, SORT—see page 34.

LEARN, TEACH—see page 57.

LIE, LAY—see page 57.

LIKE, AS
In the sentence "Winstons taste good like a cigarette should," the word "like" is used as a conjunction introducing the clause "like a cigarette should." "Like" has been used in a similar manner by many writers, including Shakespeare and his predecessors. It was used as a shortened form of the phrase "like as": "Like as a father pitieth his children. . . ." Gradually it began to be used as a substitute for "as," "as if," and "as though."

He ran *like* he had never run before.
He ran *as* he had never run before.
It looks *like* it will rain tomorrow.
It looks *as if* it will rain tomorrow.

The use of "like" as a conjunction has increased in recent years and is especially popular in speech. Such a use is still controversial, however, especially in writing. Careful speakers and writers would be wise to avoid this usage.

"Like," of course, is perfectly acceptable when used as a preposition:

Some American writers, *like* Mark Twain and Ernest Hemingway, have been very popular in other countries.
She looks *like* an angel.

NOT ONLY . . . BUT ALSO
Care should be taken with this construction to keep the two completions that follow in strict parallel order.

She came prepared *not only to sing, but also to dance.* (not: She not only came to sing, but also to dance.)

Scouting is very helpful *not only* to build up confidence and self-reliance, *but also* to encourage self-discipline and cooperation. (not: Scouting is very helpful not only to build up confidence and self-reliance, but also in encouraging self-discipline and cooperation.)

OF—see page 58.

OFF, FROM, OFF OF
1 With verbs like "take" or "borrow," the preposition that follows should be "from," not "off" or "off of."

   I borrowed a few dollars from my father. (not: I borrowed a few bucks off [of] my old man.)

2 In the expression "off of," the "of" is unnecessary.

  The milk bottle fell *off* the shelf. (not: *off of* the shelf)

ONLY—see page 71.

PREPOSITIONS ENDING SENTENCES
Early grammarians in the eighteenth century formulated the rule that sentences should never end with a preposition, and argued that because Latin did not permit it, neither should English. They argued that since the words were *prepositions* (having a position in front of), and since they couldn't be in front of anything at the end of a sentence, then such a use was wrong. Obviously, such a rule is wrong. Good writers have been effectively ending sentences with prepositions for hundreds of years. Grammatically there is nothing wrong with this practice. In fact, the original rule forces writers to change natural sentences to clumsy, awkward constructions.

Natural
Tell me what you object to.
That's the worst nonsense I have ever heard of.
What is he talking about?

Awkward
Tell me to what you object.
That is the worst nonsense of which I have ever heard.
About what is he talking?

There is a stylistic problem, however, with the indiscriminate use of prepositions at the end of sentences.

Where is he? (not: Where is he at? The preposition "at" is not needed.)
Why did you give him that knife to play with? (not: What did you give him that knife to play with for?)

Since the last position in a sentence can be a very important one, it is advisable to fill it with a word you want to stress. The word that reaches the hearer or reader last is the one that lingers. If you were emphasizing in a sentence that a murder had been committed, the first of the following two sentences would obviously be more emphatic.

This is the room in which he was murdered.
This is the room he was murdered in.

PRINCIPAL, PRINCIPLE—see page 36.

REAL—see page 71.

REGARDLESS
The word is "regardless," not "irregardless."

In many words like "irrelevant," "irreligious," "irrecoverable," the prefix "ir" has a negative effect on the root or stem. The suffix "less" has the same negative effect in words like "humorless" and "meaningless." There is no need, therefore, to place both a negative prefix and suffix around the stem word "regard."

He will come anyway, *regardless* of the consequences. (not: irregardless)

Speech bubble: *What did you bring that book that I didn't want to be read to out of up for?*

SO, SO THAT

In clauses of reason or result, use "so that" rather than the simple "so."

The coach drew a diagram of the play *so that* his players could see their mistake. (not: so his players could see their mistake)
Sidney Carton was prepared to give up his life *so that* his friend might live. (not: so his friend might live)

THEY'RE, THEIR, THERE

"They're" is the contraction for "they are"; "their" is used to show possession; "there" is used as an adverb of place.

They're lost without *their* radio.
My radio is over *there*.

THERE, HERE

"There" and "here" should not be used with the adjectives "that" and "this."

This (that) money is stolen property. (not: this here or that there money)

WHO, WHOM

When used as the object of a verb or a preposition, "who" inflects and becomes "whom." With respect to inflection, "who" behaves like the personal pronouns by having two forms (I, me; she, her; he, him; they, them; who, whom). However, "who" is not a personal pronoun; rather it belongs to another class, namely, the relative pronouns—who, which, that—a class that does not show inflection. Therefore, "who" seems to be under some pressure from these

RISE, RAISE—see page 58.

SIT, SET—see page 58.

other uninflected relative pronouns to drop its inflection. And so common practice now dictates that "who" may be used instead of "whom" except where it immediately follows a preposition.

Who (or *whom*) did you say you spoke to just now?
To *whom* did you say you spoke just now?
I don't know the man *who* (or *whom*) they elected as president.

WHICH
Make sure that the relative pronoun "which" has a specific reference or antecedent. "Which" should not be used to refer back to a whole sentence.

Today the boy replaced the ring which he stole from the store yesterday. (not: Today the boy stole a ring, which he does all the time.)

WHO'S, WHOSE
"Who's" is the contraction for "who is"; "whose" is used to show possession.

Whose woods these are I think I know. (not: who's woods)
Who's in the woods? (not: Whose in the woods?)

Splitting an infinitive

SENTENCE
SENSE

Which notes fall on the lines of the musical staff?

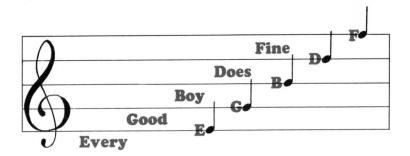

Name the royal families of England in chronological order.

No	Norman
Plan	Plantagenet
Like	Lancaster
Yours	York
To	Tudor
Study	Stuart
History	Hannover
Well	Windsor

What is your new telephone number?

Under an evergreen tree, two ate and eleven got sick.
EVergreen 2-8116

CHUNKING AND SENTENCES

Why would a music instructor teach the notes on the staff with the sentence, "Every good boy does fine"? After all, what is so hard about remembering "E, G, B, D, F"? Is it really easier to remember the order of England's royal families with the line, "No plan like yours to study history well," than it is to recall the list alone? And are you more likely to remember a phone number which spells out a word or reminds you of a nonsense line than you are to recall the numbers only? Apparently you are, and teachers and advertisers have been smart to realize the value of such memory devices. Even a nonsense line is easier for most people to remember than a sequence of meaningless numbers or letters.

WHEN THE GREEKS WERE DEVELOPING THEIR WRITING SYSTEM OVER 5000 YEARS AGO IT DID NOT OCCUR TO THEM TO USE SOME OF THE CONVENTIONS WE NOW TAKE FOR GRANTED THEY DID NOT FOR INSTANCE HAVE ANY LOWER CASE LETTERS ONLY UPPER CASE NEITHER DID THEY HAVE ANY PUNCTUATION MARKS WORSE STILL THEY ALLOWED NO SPACES BETWEEN LETTERS RATHER THEY CRAMMED ALL THE WORDS TOGETHER IN ONE CONTINUOUS SEQUENCE

Were you able to read the last half of page 109 easily? Here is the same passage in modern print.

When the Greeks were developing their writing system over 5000 years ago, it did not occur to them to use some of the conventions we now take for granted. They did not, for instance, have any lower case letters, only upper case. Neither did they have any punctuation marks. Worse still, they allowed no spaces between letters; rather they crammed all the words together in one continuous sequence.

Imagine what would happen to your reading speed if you had to struggle with this kind of system today. In what ways is our writing system closer to the rhythm of natural speech than the one used by early Greek manuscript writers?

Psychologists tell us that most human beings tend to organize information into "chunks" for easier recall. Whether it is license plate numbers or telephone numbers, we always tend to divide the meaningless sequence into groups. It is easier to remember a series of numbers like 9283228 as nine twenty-eight dash thirty-two twenty-eight. People are even happy to pay extra money for license plates which spell out certain messages, not only because they are humorous, but also because they are easier to remember.

Sentences do the same in speech. They chunk the speech flow into units which can be more easily interpreted. Good readers and good speakers are those who use the chunking process most effectively. A young child who is learning to read usually reads word by word, and in doing so, both he and his audience often lose track of the meaning of the whole passage. An

experienced reader always reads sentence by sentence. The sentence, then, is the basic unit, or chunk, in written or oral communication.

What then makes up a sentence? Many grammarians down through the ages have defined this basic unit in various ways. Look at these examples and see how you react to some of the definitions. Try making up a definition of your own. Does it vary in any way from some of these examples?

(Monge alle ...
... ke in a man the first an...
...eth not ne dredth to displese...
... the peple by lyyng disord...
nor taketh hede vnto them the...
ces. But sleeth them. In suck...
...ow. Which did so slee his ma...

1 "A sentence is an assemblage of words, expressed in proper form, ranged in proper order, and concurring to make a complete sense."

Robert Lowth, 1762

2 "Each sentence is an independent linguistic form, not included by virtue of any grammatical construction in any larger linguistic form."

Leonard Bloomfield, 1933

ames Ra...

3 "A sentence is a complete and independent utterance — the completeness and independence being shown by . . . its capability of standing alone."

Otto Jespersen, 1924

4 . . . a group of words containing a subject and a predicate."
Standard College Dictionary, 1963

5 "Sentences in English develop about patterns . . . in which a subject introduces a topic, and a verb and usually a complement comment on it."
Modern English Handbook, 1963

WORD STRINGS AND SENTENCES

When you study most subjects for the first time, you are obviously learning something new. In your study of history, geography or natural science, you are constantly learning things that you may not have known before. Grammar, however, is really quite different. You began your study of grammar as a child when you first learned to speak in sentences at about the age of two. By now you probably know a great deal about sentence structure. In fact, you could not communicate with other human beings if you did not know how to speak or write in sentences.

Since you use sentences all the time, you must, in some sense, already know what a sentence is. If you already know how to use sentences, then why study about them? There are two possible answers to this question. See how you would complete the two following statements, and discuss them with your classmates:

a Although you use sentences all the time, you may not know_____a sentence is.
b Although you use sentences whenever you speak or write, you may not always use them _____.

Learning about sentence structure is of practical use, because it can help us to avoid the common errors we all tend to make when speaking or writing in English. And, in so doing, we can make what we say or write—our communication— much more effective.

In addition, it is interesting to discover how much we already know about sentences without

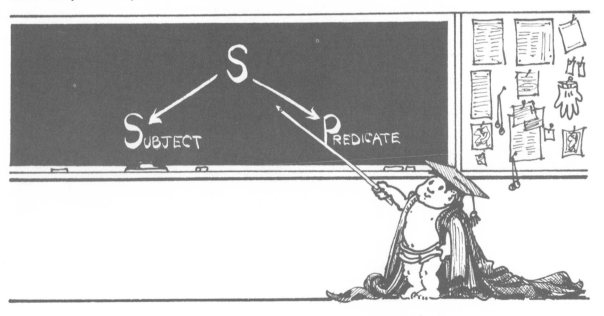

perhaps being fully aware of it. In order to prove this claim about your knowledge of sentences, let us try an experiment. How would you describe a sentence? Let's take a perfectly obvious statement and say that *a sentence is a string of words which are spoken or written one after another.* The observation is so obvious that we may not have ever thought about it in just this way before.

Definition I: *A sentence is a string of words.*

But is this definition adequate? Is it true that all strings of words are sentences? Drawing on what you already know about grammar, discuss these strings of words and see what observations you can come up with.

1 a Sentence a string is words of a.
  b A sentence is a string of words.

2 a The cauliflower sang a false tune.
  b Tune the sang cauliflower false a.

3 a John spoke to the happy.
  b John spoke to the happy audience.

4 a When I came in the door.
  b When I came in the door, he hit me in the face with a lemon pie.
  c He hit me in the face with a lemon pie when I.

In accord with our first definition, all of these examples are strings of words. From your knowledge of grammar, you probably decided that some of these strings were not sentences, while others were. How did you know? Obviously you could already tell the difference between those

examples that were merely strings of words and those which qualified as real sentences. You could not have made this distinction if you had not already known about English grammar and sentence structure.

Definition I, then, is not adequate because it cannot distinguish between strings of words that are sentences and those which are non-sentences. How might we rephrase that definition? If we look back to example 1 (a), we see that it does not make any sense. We could reword our first definition, then, as follows:

Definition II: *A sentence is a string of words that make sense.*

Example 1 (b) makes sense even though it may not be completely true. Must a sentence be a true statement? No, for we can use sentences just as easily to lie as to tell the truth. But must a statement make sense to qualify as a sentence? There does seem to be an important difference between examples 2 (a) and 2 (b). Neither of them seems to make sense, but one sounds a good deal more like an English sentence than the other. Although the meaning of 2 (a) is unusual, it does have a structure which makes it sound like an English sentence, whereas 2 (b) does not. Sense or meaning alone, therefore, cannot distinguish between those word strings which are sentences and those which are non-sentences. And thus, Definition II must be rejected.

There is something very important about the structure of sentences which seems to be missing in Definitions I and II. Discuss the following examples with your classmates; what is wrong with these "sentences"?

The angry spoke to the frightened child.
Mary opened the.
The Chicago defenseman raised.

Because of your knowledge of grammar, you would probably never write or speak in a way similar to these examples above. Why? What is wrong with these statements? How would you correct them?

When you corrected the examples above, you noticed, first of all, that the difficulty was located in a certain part of the sentence. We can sort out the problem areas in these sentences as follows:

Acceptable section	*Problem section*
spoke to the frightened child	The angry
Mary opened	the
The Chicago defenseman	raised

The words in each of the problem sections do not seem to fall into a *natural group*. When you corrected the sentences, you turned each of the problem sections into some kind of natural group such as:

The angry parents / spoke to the frightened child.
Mary opened / the door.
The Chicago defenseman / raised his hockey stick.

A sentence, then, is more than just a string of words following one after another. The words within a sentence are organized into natural groups; and, because we speak English, we can recognize that a collection of words such as "the angry teacher" is a natural group, while a sequence such as "teacher the angry" is not.

We can now modify our earlier definitions to read more accurately as follows:

Definition III: *A sentence is a string of words that fall into natural groups.*

Refer back to examples 1–4 and explain in the light of this definition what is wrong with the non-sentences.

NATURAL GROUPS

Sentences are structured word strings that fall into natural groups. But what is a natural group? If we take a fairly simple example, we will quickly discover that some groups are more natural than others.

An enraged spectator attacked the defenseless speaker.

Divide the sentence into various groupings, and discuss which of them you find acceptable and which you do not. Here are some possibilities·

An enraged
enraged spectator
attacked the defenseless speaker
the defenseless
An enraged spectator
spectator attacked the
attacked the defenseless
the defenseless speaker

Of these and other possibilities, which seem to be natural groupings and which do not? To simplify the analysis, divide the single sentence into two main groups. Here are three of six possibilities. What do you think of them? Remember, each half must form a natural group.

An enraged spectator attacked the/
defenseless speaker.
An enraged/spectator attacked
the defenseless speaker.
An enraged spectator attacked the
defenseless/speaker.

Where would you make the division so that the sentence falls into two natural groups?
Perhaps the easiest way to visualize this notion of natural groups is to use a *tree-diagram*. In dividing the sample sentence, most speakers would make the following separation:

An enraged spectator/attacked the defenseless speaker.

We can transpose this to a tree-diagram as follows:

The first half of the sentence is called the *sub-ject* and tells us who or what did the action; the second half is called the *predicate* and tells us what action was performed. But we can go further than this. We can divide each half as well. Starting with the predicate, we can separate the verb from its *direct object*, which tells us who or what was the object of the action.

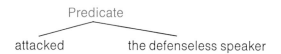

So far we have made these divisions:

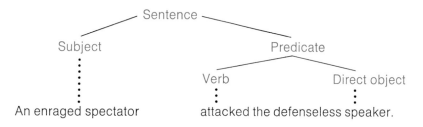

We are now left with two identical noun phrases, one of which is the subject of the sentence, and the other, the direct object of the verb. Both can be subdivided in two further stages:

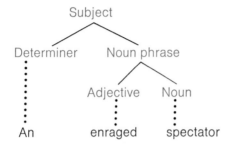

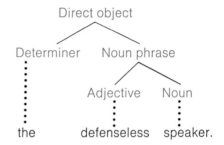

Putting it all together on a tree-diagram, we obtain the following:

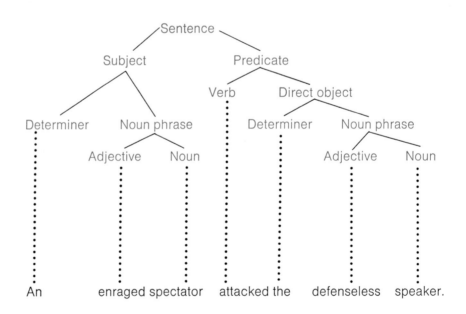

The tree-diagram can apply to a wide variety of different sentences which all fall into the same natural groups, such as:

That little child eats a special diet.
The charging gorilla beat his hairy chest.
Seventy-six angry trombones outplayed the startled musicians.

Draw a tree-diagram for any one of these three sentences.

All sentences, then, are made up of natural groups that show the structural relationships between various parts of the sentence. All sentences have a subject and a predicate. The subject may consist of a subject noun phrase. The direct object may be part of an object noun phrase.

Predicates may be varied to form different patterns. What we have seen thus far is the *verb / object pattern.* Consider now some of these other possibilities:

Verb / Indirect object / Direct object

The *indirect object* tells us to whom or for whom the action was done. To check for an indirect object, place "to" or "for" in front of the word and see whether it makes sense. For example, "Mary gave (to) the boy her ring," or "Al bought (for) his brother a tie."

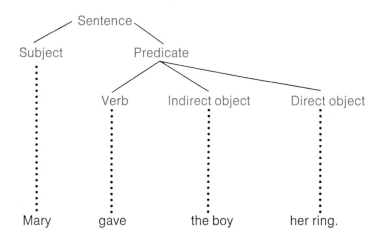

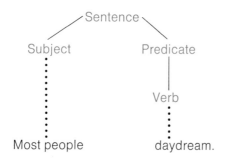

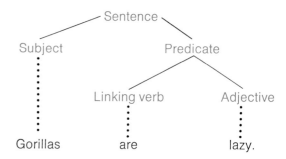

Although there are other patterns as well as these, the main point to remember is that all sentences fall into natural groups that show the structural relationship between different parts of the sentence. As you read or hear a properly formed sentence, you automatically make these groupings; if you cannot make the sentence fall into natural groups, chances are that the string of words is not a sentence.

activities

1 In the ambiguous sentence, "Mary fed her dog biscuits," the phrase "her dog biscuits" can be grouped in two different ways—"her dog/ biscuits" meaning Mary fed biscuits to her dog, or "her/dog biscuits" meaning Mary fed dog biscuits to someone. In the following sentences, show how certain strings of words can be grouped to mean different things.

a The rock singer turned on his audience.
b I can see the book ends in the middle there.
c Vegetarians don't know how good meat tastes.

2 In each of the following pairs, identify the string of words which has the structure of an English sentence. Does a sentence have to make sense to qualify as a sentence?

a The nets swam merrily in the afternoon tea.
  In merrily the tea afternoon the swam nets.

b The morning sun in ate summer their dande-lions the tulips.
  In the morning sun the tulips ate their summer dandelions.

c Well and their did rulers erasers homework.
  Rulers and erasers did their homework well.

d A chirping ant was eating the fat elephant.
  Ant elephant the eating was chirping a fat.

3 Try reading the following poem by e. e. cummings
out loud without first reading it over. Why did
you have difficulty? Why does figuring out the
sentence structure of the poem have so much to
do with figuring out the meaning of the poem?
Have several different people tape a reading
of the poem. Do they always pause for sentence
breaks in the same places?

Spring is like a perhaps hand
(which comes carefully
out of Nowhere) arranging
a window, into which people look (while
people stare
arranging and changing placing
carefully there a strange
thing and a known thing here) and

changing everything carefully

spring is like a perhaps
Hand in a window
(carefully to
and fro moving New and
Old things, while
people stare carefully
moving a perhaps
fraction of flower here placing
an inch of air there) and

without breaking anything.

e. e. cummings

119

COMMUNICATION SITUATIONS

If the sentence is the basic unit of verbal expression, why do we sometimes have difficulty with sentence structures in our own writing? There are probably two main reasons. One is that writing can put us "on the spot" in a way that we are not accustomed to in ordinary speech. When writing, we cannot rely on many of the non-verbal tricks that we frequently use in speech: those gestures that fill in awkward silences or help to clarify or highlight our meaning. Ineffective speakers will supplement expressions like "you know ah . . ." with gestures which invite us to fill in the verbal gaps. We all get stuck at times for words or expressions, and in our desperation we will often fall back on gestures which we try to make appear meaningful. When writing, we cannot rely on body movement as an aid to meaning.

The second reason for our difficulty in writing proper sentences is a more subtle one. Various communication situations raise different expectations about what kinds of sentence structures are acceptable. In speech, in advertising, in fiction, and in expository writing, differing degrees of sentence completeness are allowable.

Speech is the loosest in its requirements; in spontaneous conversation we can get by with a reasonable proportion of incomplete or abbreviated sentences. Expository writing, such as essays, magazine articles, or editorials, are examples of more formal situations which require a higher degree of completeness in sentence structure.

When we switch from one situation to another, we must be prepared to alter the kind of sentence structure we use. Naturally this jumping from one communication situation to another requires a certain amount of practice and skill, along with an awareness of the differences between situations and their requirements. The following diagram summarizes the situations which differ from one another only in degree.

Informal   *Formal*

incomplete sentences commonly expected	incomplete sentences accepted for effect	incomplete sentences accepted in dialogue	incomplete sentences rarely accepted
CONVERSATION	ADVERTISING	FICTION	EXPOSITORY WRITING
complete sentences not always expected	complete sentences accepted but not always required	complete sentences expected except in dialogue	complete sentences required except in rare cases for special effects

THE ADVERTISING SITUATION

The main purpose of advertising is to persuade individuals to buy a product or service. Persuasion is not restricted to advertising, however. Political speeches are also concerned with persuasion, but they differ from advertisements in several ways: they are longer and they rely more heavily on extended logical argument.

Advertisements have to make their point very quickly. They must capture the wandering attention of a magazine reader or television viewer and create their effect in as short a space as possible. Because language takes longer to process in the mind than pictures do, the verbal content of ads is probably less important than visual appeal. It is natural, therefore, that the language of advertising should favor an abbreviated style. Consider the following sentence fragments from magazine advertisements for a Harley-Davidson motorcycle. Then discuss the questions below.

Out where the best begins.

Getting it all together.

The Great American Freedom Machine.

a Each of the statements is an incomplete sentence structure. Without the rest of the accompanying ad, do these statements make sense?

b Each of the statements is in boldface (heavy) type. Why? Do these statements name products or make assertions?

c Why is each of these statements punctuated with a period as if it were a full sentence?

Some of our best hamburger salesmen

And Filet O' Fish salesmen.
And Big Mac salesmen.
And Quarter Pounder™ salesmen.
McDonald's famous french fries.
Hot. Crisp. And golden.
Never has a potato
done so much for so many.

*Pre cooked weight 1/4 lb.

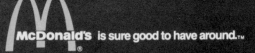

McDonald's is sure good to have around.™

Because of the visual element in advertising, language does not have to do all of the work in the total communication act. Frequently the name of a product serves as an indicator of the "topic," or subject, of the sentence. The predicate part of the sentence, which presents certain attitudes or supplies some information, can then be given in the form of printed words. Study the McDonald's advertisement on page 122.

a Which part of the total sentence is provided by the picture and which part by the printed words? Would one part make sense without the other?

b Which element is more important—the visual or the verbal?

c What effect does the presence of visual content have on the need to make statements in the form of complete sentences? If the verbal message were in the form of complete sentences, would the total message be more or less effective?

d In what way does the "reader" of an advertisement have to work differently than when he is reading ordinary (connected) prose? Is it more difficult to read a statement in connected prose or an advertisement using both print and pictures?

Some advertisements are highly visual in total effect, while others rely more heavily on language. Are the language and the sentence structures used in written advertisements different from the language and style of connected prose? Consider, for instance, the following advertisement. Pay particular attention to the sentence structure.

That little thing next to the mouse is a computer. And it doesn't bite.

It costs a lot less than a big computer. So instead of putting it up on a pedestal, you can afford to put it to work.

You can move it to where the work is. On the production line. In the lab. Classrooms. Offices.

It's tough enough to work where it's too cold for people to work. Or too hot.

And it can tolerate double the voltage reduction of a big computer. So it's less likely to blow out in case of a brownout.

This computer is one of many made by Data General. The fastest growing maker of small computers in the world today.

Write for our brochure: "The Sensible Way To Look At Computers."

It may be just the thing you need to scare you into buying one of ours.

DataGeneral
The computer company you can understand.

Data General Corporation, Dept. C, Southboro, Massachusetts 01772, (617) 485-9100.
Datagen of Canada Ltd., Hull, Quebec (819) 770-2030/Data General Europe, Paris, France 504-23-44

a Why are the sentences at the beginning and the end more complete than those in the middle?

b Study paragraphs two and three. Expand each of the incomplete sentences into complete statements. Why is the shorter form preferable for the ad?

c Why does the ad copy use so many brief paragraphs? How would the ad look if printed in a single block paragraph? Why, in paragraph form, is a single sentence given one whole paragraph?

Obviously, the familiar conventions of connected prose are greatly relaxed in writing advertising copy. Incomplete sentences, variation in print type and print size, the multiplication of short paragraphs and the reliance on visual content— all these techniques are used to create a more informal communication style. Frequent use of incomplete sentences helps the advertiser to achieve greater immediate impact. Compared to conventional connected prose, advertising copy is much less formal, certainly more fragmentary, and therefore more similar to the language of colloquial speech.

activity

You are a junior copywriter for a well-known advertising company. You have just submitted the following advertising copy to your senior editor. He tells you that the ad is too long and too formal in tone. He wants you to reword the message by shortening it and using incomplete sentence fragments rather than full sentences. Submit your revised draft to the class.

In a world of artificial smiles and paper-thin walls, Hotel Vancouver is an oasis. It is elegant and gracious. It is dedicated to fine personal service and yet it is discreetly modernized to offer our guests every creature comfort. We are an oasis, and we are where an oasis should be. We are in the very center of the city, just a few time-saving steps to wherever your business takes you. You will find four of Vancouver's best restaurants here and most of Vancouver's most distinguished visitors. These visitors are people like you whose standards are as demanding as our own. Remember the name now, Hotel Vancouver. They do not build hotels like this any more today, but maybe they should.

Turn to page 127 for the actual ad.

THE SPEECH SITUATION

Most speech situations call for an informal sentence style. In ordinary conversation, we tend to use incomplete sentences more frequently than in writing. Young children have more difficulty with sentence structure than adults. Consider this version of the story of Niobe which is told by a child who is seven years old.

There's once a lady who's called Niobe, and she had twelve sons and twelve daughters . . . and there's a fairy who had one son and no daughters . . . uhm . . . then Niobe laughed at the fairy because she only . . . she had only one son, and she had twelve sons and twelve daughters. Then, at this, she got mad and fastened her to a rock. Ten years went by and she . . . her tears . . . she cried. Then she turned into a rock, and now today her tears are . . . in the river . . . flowing in a river.

The young speaker assumes that the listener knows who the "she" is at all times, but, of course, the listener does not. If the listener and the speaker do not share the same background information, faulty communication may occur. For the correct version of the story turn to page 126.

For the correct version of the story turn to page 126.

In case you think adults are always much clearer in their sentence structure than children are, consider this verbal salad—the actual com-

As far as I know, no one yet has done the in a way obvious now and interesting problem of doing a in a sense structural frequency study of the alternative syntactical in a given language, say like English, the alternative possible structures, and how what their hierarchical probability of occurrence structure is.

ment made by a speaker at a conference of linguists and psychologists.

The adult's speech makes use of bigger words, of course, but is the sentence structure really any better—or is it worse—than the child's? Presumably this speaker would never write a sentence like that, but under the pressure of trying to think on his feet in public, his thoughts seem to be racing ahead of his sentence structure. When we are thinking through an idea for the first time, particularly if we are under pressure, our sentence structure frequently suffers.

© 1967 United Features Syndicate, Inc.

activities

1 Mental confusion is often reflected by distortion in sentence structure. Tape a sample section from a radio phone-in talk program or a TV talk show on a controversial subject. Notice particularly the occurrence of incomplete or confused sentence structure. What is the relationship between a speaker's sentence structure and his mental and emotional condition? Why are intense emotions such as rage often uncommunicable in verbal terms?

2 Young writers are often advised to write the way they would speak. Why is this both good and bad advice?

Following is the original version of the Niobe story referred to on page 133, from *The Language and Thought of the Child,* by Jean Piaget.

Once upon a time, there was a lady called Niobe, who had twelve sons and twelve daughters. She met a fairy who had only one son and no daughters at all. The lady laughed at the fairy because the fairy had only one boy. When this happened, the fairly became very angry and fastened the lady to a rock. The poor lady cried for ten years. Eventually she turned into a rock, and her tears made a stream which still runs today.

In a world of artificial smiles and paper-thin walls, Hotel Vancouver is an oasis. Elegant. Gracious. Dedicated to fine personal service. Yet discreetly modernized to offer our guests every creature comfort.

And we're where an oasis should be. In the very center of the city, a few time-saving steps to wherever your business or pleasure takes you.

You'll find four of Vancouver's best restaurants here. And most of Vancouver's most distinguished visitors—people like you whose standards are as demanding as our own.

Hotel Vancouver. They don't build hotels like this any more. Maybe they should.

There will always be a few hotels like this.

Hotel Vancouver is a CN Hotel operated by Hilton Canada. Free garage parking for registered guests. Colour TV. Other Hilton-operated hotels in Canada: The Queen Elizabeth, Montreal (a CN Hotel), the Montréal Aéroport Hilton, Toronto Airport Hilton and Québec Hilton (opening this year). For reservations call your travel agent, any Hilton or CN Hotel or Hilton Reservation Service.

THE WRITING SITUATION

We have suggested that the speech and the advertising situations are more informal than the writing situation and thus more tolerant of incomplete sentences. Does this mean that writers should always avoid incomplete sentence structures? Notice, for example, the highly abbreviated sentences used by these two characters in Dickens' *Tale of Two Cities:*

"How goes it, Jacques?"
"All well, Jacques."
"Touch then!"
They joined hands, and the man sat down on the heap of stones.
"No dinner?"
"Nothing but supper now," said the mender of roads, with a hungry face.
"It is the fashion," growled the man. "I meet no dinner anywhere."

The effect is ominous. Little is said, much implied but left unspoken. It could be argued, of course, that Dickens was trying to reproduce in this written passage the informality of spoken conversation. In fiction, a writer will often attempt to reproduce the informality of the speech situation, incomplete sentences and all. Fiction generally is much more tolerant than exposition of the use of incomplete sentences.

Compare the following two passages. The first is from a novel by Sheila Watson, *The Double Hook.* Her descriptive style is highly poetic and much more inclined to the use of incomplete sentences than the explanatory style of the second passage, which is from Samuel Hearne's *Coppermine Journey.*

At last he came to the pole fence of the Indian reservation. The cabins huddled together. Wheels without wagons. Wagons without wheels. Bits of harness. Rags and tatters of clothing strung up like fish greyed over with death. He saw the bone-thin dogs. Waiting. Heard them yelping, saw them running to drive him off territory they'd been afraid to defend. Snarling. Twisting. Tumbling away from the heels they pursued.

From *The Double Hook,* by Sheila Watson

While we lay in ambush, the Indians performed the last ceremonies which were thought necessary before the engagement. These chiefly consisted in painting their faces, some all black, some all red, and others a mixture of the two. And to prevent their hair from blowing into their eyes, it was either tied before and behind and on both sides, or else cut short all round. The next thing they considered was to make themselves as light as possible for running, which they did by pulling off their stockings and either cutting off the sleeves of their jackets or rolling them up close to their armpits.

From *Coppermine Journey,* by Samuel Hearne

Why does the subject matter of the first passage lend itself more readily to informal abbreviated sentence structure than that of the second? Try rewriting the first passage by Sheila Watson in complete sentence form. How are the feeling and rhythm affected? In what way is this passage similar to the advertising copy on page 123?

Sometimes a fiction writer will use incomplete or abbreviated sentence structure to create a certain effect. In what way(s) does the structure of this next passage add to the feeling of what is being said?

I can smell the Antelope in the Sky. Treading on soft tongues of snow plant. Moving many times through the trees. Always the trees. It is the way of my people. Close to their animal skin, the hide tight on their bodies; I can smell. Can smell wet wood. Underneath a cut pile, after snows are melted, rains are gone, the bottom pieces with faces pressed in damp Earth. Faces covered with mildew. That is their smell. The smell of gray fibers growing softly. Thickly into a mask. Masks moving in the Sky. Brown bodies turning. Watching peacefully as I stalk. I am sly. I am swift. I am the one to apprehend them. Waiting to allow me passage. Slipping my knife into their Spirits. Cutting the meat from their sides. I am the boss of them that allow me to feast, to grow. I am strong boss of my people. Not a leader. A boss of Antelope hunts. I am the Antelope Boss. The one to point the way. To direct a finger at the Sky.

From *Rabbit Boss*, by Thomas Sanchez

Most magazine articles, newspaper editorials, textbooks, encyclopedias, and other information sources tend to use a writing style that relies almost exclusively on complete sentence structures. Since all of these are examples of expository writing, it would be natural to conclude that exposition rarely makes use of incomplete sentences; certainly it does not to the extent that novels and short stories sometimes do. Expository writing is normally a more formal type of writing than narrative fiction, and its style usually favors the more formal structure of the complete sentence form.

But there are exceptions to this generalization. Consider the next two examples. They are non-fiction journal or diary entries. Notice the heavy use of incomplete sentences. The first is a description of the fire of London by the famous seventeenth century writer, Samuel Pepys.

September 2, 1666—Having seen as much as I could now, I away to White Hall by appointment, and there walked to St. James's Park; and there met my wife, and Creed, and Wood, and his wife, and walked to my boat; and there upon the water again, and to the fire up and down, it still increasing, and the wind great. So near the fire as we could for smoke; and all over the Thames, with one's face in the wind, you were almost burned with a shower of fire-drops. This is very true: so as houses were burned by these drops and flakes of fire, three or four, nay, five or six houses, one from another. When we could endure no more upon the water, we to a little alehouse on the Bankside, over against the Three Cranes, and there staid 'till it was dark almost, and saw the fire grow; and, as it grew darker, appeared more and more; and in corners and upon steeples, and between churches and houses, as far as we could see up the hill of the City, in a most horrid, malicious, bloody flame, not like the fine flame of an ordinary fire. We staid till, it being darkish, we saw the fire as only one entire arch of fire from this to the other side the bridge, and in a bow up the hill for an arch of above a mile long: it made me weep to see it. The churches, houses, and all on fire, and flaming at once; and a horrid noise the flames made, and the cracking of houses at their ruine. So home with a sad heart.

From *The Diary of Samuel Pepys*

The second example is from the journal of the famous Antarctic explorer, R. F. Scott. It consists of his last entries before death overtook him and his fellow explorers just eleven miles from his base camp.

Wednesday, March 21, 1912—Got within 11 miles of depot Monday night; had to lay up all yesterday in severe blizzard. To-day forlorn hope, Wilson and Bowers going to depot for fuel.

Thursday, March 22 and 23—Blizzard bad as ever—Wilson and Bowers unable to start—to-morrow last chance—no fuel and only one or two of food left—must be near the end. Have decided it shall be natural—we shall march for the depot with or without our effects and die in our tracks.

Thursday, March 29—Since the 21st have had continuous gale from W.S.W. and S.W. We had fuel to make two cups of tea apiece and bare food for two days on the 20th. Every day have been ready to start for our depot 11 miles away, but outside the door of the tent a scene of whirling drift. Do not think we can hope for any better things now. Shall stick it out to the end, but are getting weaker, of course, and the end cannot be far.

It seems a pity, but I do not think I can write more.

Last entry—For God's sake look after our people.

From *Scott's Last Expedition*

130

Why do you think the journal or diary writer tends to a more telegraphic style? What parts of speech or parts of sentences did the writer tend to omit? Could you understand the sentences in all cases even with the parts omitted? Since most diary or journal entries are fairly short, the writer usually can get away with a rather telegraphic form of writing. Could a novelist write this way, do you think, over several hundred pages? Why might it get rather difficult to read after a while?

The following humorous tale comes from the lore of the Old West. After reading the entire story, choose two paragraphs from it and re-write them in the telegraphic style of the diary or journal examples you have seen in the preceding pages. Shorten the sentences by leaving out some words and parts of whole sentences.

I was never frightened but once during all my travels in the mountains. That was in the winter of 1857. I was crossing Hope Valley, when I came to a place where six great wolves—big timber wolves—were at work in the snow, digging out the carcass of some animal. Now, in my childhood in Norway, I had heard so many stories about the ferocity of wolves that I feared them more than any other wild animal. To my eyes, those before me looked to have hair on them a foot long. They were great, gaunt, shaggy fellows. My course lay near them. I knew I must show a bold front. All my life I had heard that the wolf—savage and cruel as he is—seldom has the courage to attack anything that does not run at his approach. I might easily run from bears, but these were customers of a different kind. There was nothing of them but bones, sinews, and hair. They could skim over the snow like birds.

As I approached, the wolves left the carcass, and in single file came out a distance of about twenty-five yards toward my line of march. The leader of the pack then wheeled about and sat down on his haunches. When the next one came up he did the same, and so on, until all were seated in a line. They acted just like trained soldiers. I pledge you my word, I thought the devil was in them! There they sat, every eye and every sharp nose turned toward me as I approached. In the old country, I had heard of 'man-wolves,' and these acted as if of that supernatural kind. To look at them gave me cold chills, and I had a queer feeling about the roots of my hair. What most frightened me was the confidence they displayed, and the regular order in which they moved. But I dared not show the least sign of fear, as on I went.

Just when I was opposite them, and but twenty-five or thirty yards away, the leader of the pack threw back his head and uttered a long and prolonged howl. All the others of the pack did the same. "Ya-hoo-oo! Ya-oo, woo-oo!" cried all together. A more doleful and terrific sound I never heard. I thought it meant my death. The awful cry rang across the silent valley, was echoed by the hills, and re-echoed far away among the surrounding mountains.

Every moment I expected to see the whole pack dash at me. I would just then have given all I possessed to have had my revolver in my hand. However, I did not alter my gait nor change my line of march. I passed the file of wolves as a general moves along in front of his soldiers. The ugly brutes uttered but their first fearful howl. When they saw that their war-cry did not cause me to alter my course nor make me run, they feared to come after me; so they let me pass.

They sat still and watched me hungrily for some time, but when I was far away, I saw them all turn about and go back to the carcass. Had I turned back or tried to run away when they marched out to meet me, I am confident the whole pack would have been upon me in a moment. They all looked it. My *show* of courage intimidated them and kept them back.

From "Snowshoe Thompson," by Dan De Quille

CONCLUSION

Sentences are the major chunking units. Of speech.
And of writing.
Sentences are strings of words. Which fall into ·
natural groups.

Complete sentences always have a subject. And predicate.
The subject may be a subject noun phrase. The direct object
may be part of an object noun phrase. Predicates may have
different patterns. Such as:
   verb/direct object.
   verb/indirect object/direct object.
   intransitive verb (no object).
   linking verb/adjective.
And other patterns as well.

Not all sentences in a communication need
necessarily be complete.
Incomplete sentences are fairly common in the
speech situation. And also in the advertising situation.

In writing, incomplete sentences are less
frequently tolerated. Except in reported dialogue.
In expository writing, incomplete sentences are
rarely tolerated. Except in "telegraphic writing." Such
as student notes. Or telegrams. Or some kinds of diary and
journal entries.

When writing incomplete sentences, make sure the reader
can fill in the meaning from the context. Otherwise a
breakdown in communication will result.

This message will self-destruct in sixty seconds.
Starting now.
Unless you rewrite this passage in connected prose.

SENTENCE
COMBINING

LINKING AND INSERTING PROCESSES

In the last chapter we defined a sentence as a string of words that fall into natural groups. A simple sentence had, we observed, a subject and a predicate, and these were the two basic units common to all simple sentences. In this chapter we want to observe the ways in which two simple sentences may be combined to form another sentence which has a more complex structure.

Consider the two columns below. Each sentence in both columns is a simple sentence. Join the sentence in Column 1 with its partner in Column 2 to form one combined sentence. See how many ways you can combine each part. You should be able to find at least two different ways for each.

Column 1	Column 2
John loves Mary.	Mary isn't interested in John.
It may rain tomorrow.	We will have to cancel the picnic.
Curtis pitched a fine game.	His team lost again.
The thief ducked into the subway train.	The doors closed immediately on his pursuers.
The Chevy was originally mine.	Now it belongs to my brother.

Your experimenting should lead you to discover two basic patterns which are available to you.

An easy way to see these two combining processes is by studying the following diagrams.

Linking process

| Simple Sentence 1, | { and, or, but, yet } | Simple Sentence 2 | = | Compound Sentence |

Inserting process

| { When, If, Although, Because, etc. } | Simple Sentence 1, | Simple Sentence 2 | = | Complex Sentence |

Now using the examples from Columns 1 and 2, we get these two basic patterns:

Linking process

John loves Mary, *but* she isn't interested in John.
It may rain tomorrow, *and* we will have to cancel the picnic.
Curtis pitched a fine game, *but* his team lost again.
The thief ducked into the subway train, *and* the doors closed immediately on his pursuers.
The Chevy was originally mine, *but* now it belongs to my brother.

Inserting process

Although John loves Mary, she isn't interested in him.
If it rains tomorrow, we will have to cancel the picnic.
Even though Curtis pitched a fine game, his team lost again.
When the thief ducked into the subway train, the doors closed immediately on his pursuers.
The Chevy *that* was originally mine now belongs to my brother.

Both the linking and the inserting processes keep the essential content of each combining part, but there is a difference in the structure of the resulting sentence. What is it? As a clue, try reading alone that part which was originally labeled Sentence 1 in your new combined sentence.

Compare, for instance,

John loves Mary

with

Although John loves Mary

Do you notice any difference in the ability of either grouping to stand alone? Check out all of the examples under *Inserting process*. Notice that, because of the introductory word (*although, if, even though, when, that*), the section which was originally Sentence 1 is now no longer independent. In other words, the inserted part of the sentence cannot stand alone. In what way is this combined structure different from the combined structure of the linking process?

The independence or dependence of the parts in the combined sentence is what makes linking and inserting different kinds of structures. When two simple sentences are linked together, we get what is called a *compound sentence.* Each part is independent and could stand alone as a sentence if separated from the other. When two simple sentences are combined by the inserting process, we obtain what is called a *complex sentence.* One part is independent and the other, inserted part(s), is dependent; the inserted one(s) cannot stand alone in written prose if separated from the main one. Compound and complex sentences are both useful structures for bringing variety into your writing.

Dear Ann Landers: I'm only the father, so, of course, I don't have anything to say around here. I am permitted to pay the bills and drive everybody where they want to go. I just keep my mouth shut and do as I'm told.

My demands are simple. All I want is a chance to look at the newspaper while it's still readable, Yesterday where your column should have been was a big hole. Our daughter tore it out to take to her family living class. Yesterday the crossword puzzle was missing. My mother-in-law wanted to do it "later." This morning my wife ripped out a recipe for peanut butter soup. On the other side were the stock-market returns which I wanted to read. If I complain, I'm "a sourpuss." What about this?
—**M.C.P.**

1 Read the letter to Ann Landers' advice column which is shown at left. Pretend that you are Ann Landers and write a brief reply. What kind of sentence structure did you rely on most heavily: simple, compound, or complex? Would a limited space for the reply have any bearing on the kind of sentence structure you would use?

2 No writer ever limits himself to a single type of sentence structure, but often a piece of writing will have a dominant recurring rhythm. Read the following examples. Then identify each sentence in them as simple, compound, complex, or compound-complex. Explain how you arrived at your answer. What sentence pattern in each passage appears most often?

a At Hanukkah time the road from the village to the town is usually covered with snow, but this year the winter had been a mild one. Hanukkah had almost come, yet little snow had fallen. The sun shone most of the time. The peasants complained that because of the dry weather there would be a poor harvest of winter grain. New grass sprouted, and the peasants sent their cattle out to pasture.

From "Zlateh the Goat," by Isaac Bashevis Singer

b He drove to the corner and looked at the street sign. It was the street, all right—Giles Avenue. He went back and checked the address. It should have been the right address. That's when he realized his building was gone.

The city had struck again. It's almost like sleight of hand. Here you own a building. Presto! Now you own a vacant lot.

From "Now You See It . . . ," by Mike Royko

c All that morning we argued our way across the Mare Crisium while the western mountains reared higher in the sky. Even when we were out prospecting in the space suits, the discussion would continue over the radio. It was absolutely certain, my companions argued, that there had never been any form of intelligent life on the moon. The only living things that had ever existed there were a few primitive plants and their slightly less degenerate ancestors. I knew that as well as anyone, but there are times when a scientist must not be afraid to make a fool of himself.

From "The Sentinel," by Arthur C. Clarke

COMMON PROBLEMS WITH COMPOUND SENTENCES

Whenever a child tells a story, it is interesting to note how heavily the youngster relies on the linking process in stringing his sentences together. Instead of inserting sentences inside other sentences, young children tend to string out one after another. One of their favorite linking expressions seems to be the phrase, "and then." Consider this example from the speech of a six-and-a-half-year-old child. Given some diagrams of a simple water tap, the young boy was asked to explain how it worked.

Here there's the pipe, and then it is opened, and then the water runs into the basin, and then there it is shut, so the water doesn't run any more, then there's the little pipe lying down, and then the basin's full of water, and the water can't run out 'cos the little pipe is there, lying down, and that stops it.

From *The Language and Thought of the Child,* by Jean Piaget

How does your sentence structure differ from that of the young child in speaking? in writing?

Whereas we would probably depend more heavily on structures such as, "when X . . . then Y," the child relies almost entirely on structures such as, "X . . . and then Y . . . then Z." The child seems able only to string his thoughts out one after another.

In many of us, the gradual growth of logical thought is reflected by the gradual development of more complex sentence structures. With age and practice, our sentence combining slowly swings from a heavy use of the sequential linking process ("and then . . . then next . . .") to a greater use of the inserting process ("if . . . then . . ."). Does this development mean that linking sentences necessarily sound immature?

Study the two following passages. They are both based fairly heavily on the linking process. Do they sound to you like the childish sentence structures illustrated in the speech of the six-and-a-half-year-old child?

The sun rose thinly from the sea and the old man could see the other boats, low on the water and well in toward the shore. . . . Then the sun was brighter and the glare came on the water and then, as it rose clear, the flat sea sent it back at his eyes so that it hurt sharply and he rowed without looking into it.

From *The Old Man and the Sea,* by Ernest Hemingway

Here is the way we put in the time. It was a monstrous big river down there; we run nights, and laid up and hid day-times; soon as night was most gone, we stopped navigating and tied up—nearly always in the dead water under a tow-head; and then cut young cotton-woods and willows and hid the raft with them. Then we set out the lines. Next we slid into the river and had a swim, so as to freshen up and cool off; then we set down on the sand bottom where the water was about knee deep, and watched the daylight come.

From *Huckleberry Finn,* by Mark Twain

In the first passage a simple old man is speaking and in the second, an illiterate young boy. Is this reason enough to explain the author's choice of sentence style? Both Hemingway and Twain are admired for their subtle literary style. But their style is a difficult one to imitate, because, when the linking process is used excessively, the style is in danger of degenerating into something very similar to that of the young child. Running a whole series of sentences together without a break is a problem that we should investigate carefully.

THE RUN-ON SENTENCE AND THE COMMA SPLICE

Imagine, for a moment, that you are an assistant in the office of the mayor of a large city. You have just received an urgent call to come down to the glass and marble lobby of your brand new City Hall. You arrive on the scene and see to your horror a mob of demonstrators consisting of one adult and sixty little children—all eating ice cream and candy and drinking pop. This is one author's description of the scene.

The young guy from the Mayor's office re-treats . . . Much consternation and concern in the lobby of City Hall . . . the hurricane could get worse. The little devils could start screaming, wailing, ululating, belching, moaning, giggling, making spook-show sounds . . . filling the very air with a hurricane of malted milk, an orange blizzard of crushed ice from the Slurpees, with acid red horrors like the red from the taffy apples and the jelly from the jelly doughnuts, with globs of ice cream in purple sheets of root beer, with plastic straws and huge bilious waxed cups and punch cans and sprinkles of Winkles, with mustard from off the hot dogs and little

lettuce shreds from off the tacos, with things that splash and things that plop and things that ooze and stick, that filthy sugar moss from off the cotton candy, and the Karamel Korn and the butterscotch daddy figures from off the Sugar-Daddies and the butterscotch babies from off the Sugar-Babies, sugar, water, goo, fried fat, droplets, driplets, shreds, bits, lumps, gums,

gobs, smears, from the most itchy molecular Winkle to the most warm moist emetic mass of Three Musketeer bar and every gradation of solubility and liquidity known to syrup—filling the air, choking it, getting trapped gurgling and spluttering in every glottis—

From *Radical Chic and Mau-Mauing the Flak Catchers,* by Tom Wolfe

Now the question is, as an English teacher, would you fail Tom Wolfe's description for faulty sentence structure? The sentence does run on, and on—and on. Is it effective for the purpose intended by the author? Does the author know what he is doing, or does he write this way because he doesn't know any better? Compare, for instance, the Tom Wolfe passage with this example:

The common factor in the development of Egypt was based around the river Nile, around the rich river valley and so they could do their cultivation of crops, the Nile overflowed about twice each period, thus making the valley's soil rich and due to the flow of the Nile provide means of transportation for them, and also because of its flow, they could be recognized by other merchants as they travel up and down the river also because of desert and mountain on both sides of the Nile served as a protection for the Egyptians, whereas in Babylon, they had no form of protection. The Euphrates and the Tigrus River was Babylon's main source of development. These two rivers having their overflow so often deposited silt on the land making the fertile crescent very rich, the same form was used we see both countries using this method which was having surplus food which they took from the people as tax.

Obviously this unfortunate writer has no idea about sentence structure. Worse still, as readers we have great difficulty in understanding what he is trying to say. Run-on sentences can be used to effect by the mature writer, but, when handled badly, as in this last example, they are a dead giveaway of real incompetence. The difference between intentional and accidental use of the run-on sentence is, to paraphrase Mark Twain, like the difference between "lightning and the lightning bug."

The problems of the run-on sentence and the comma splice have a common origin. The difficulty arises, in both cases, when a writer does not properly separate independent sentences. Study these examples and discuss various ways of correcting them:

Run-on sentence

The cowardly old bulldog scurried quickly under the porch he had just seen a harmless pussycat she was merely trying to be friendly in old Rover's brain the tiny frisky cat had somehow come to be mistaken for a fearsome roaring lion.

Comma splice

The cowardly old bulldog scurried quickly under the porch, he had just seen a harmless pussycat, she was merely trying to be friendly, in old Rover's brain the tiny, frisky cat had somehow come to be mistaken for a fearsome roaring lion.

142

How many simple sentences are there in each version? Once you have established the number of simple sentences, you must now decide how you want to present them. You have plenty of alternatives, but here are some to consider:

a   You can leave them as a string of simple sentences, but you must then punctuate each of them with a period.
b   You may wish to employ the inserting process or the linking process, in which case you may have to use commas.
c   You may wish to reduce some of the sentences to an "ing" phrase construction ("seeing a harmless pussycat").

Study these possible examples and note the punctuation.

1   The cowardly old bulldog scurried quickly under the porch. He had just seen a harmless pussycat. She was merely trying to be friendly. However, in old Rover's brain, the tiny, frisky cat had somehow come to be mistaken for a fearsome roaring lion.

2   When the cowardly old bulldog saw a harmless pussycat, he scurried quickly under the porch. She was merely trying to be friendly, but in old Rover's brain the tiny, frisky cat had somehow come to be mistaken for a fearsome roaring lion.

3   Seeing a harmless pussycat which was merely trying to be friendly, the cowardly old bulldog scurried quickly under the porch. Somehow, in old Rover's brain, the tiny, frisky cat had come to be mistaken for a fearsome roaring lion.

There are many other possible ways to organize these four simple sentences into a piece of prose. This simple rule may help you to avoid the problem of the run-on sentence and the comma splice:

a   A series of simple sentences normally should be separated from one another by something more than a comma.

b   Commas should be used in compound or complex sentences to separate linking or initial elements.

How serious for the reader are the problems of the run-on sentence and the comma splice? Normally, when reading, the eye travels across the page from left to right. When reading a passage which is studded with run-on sentences and comma splices, the eye often has to retrace its normal direction. It must go back while the brain figures out where the sentence should begin and end. This difficulty is an inconvenience to the reader; but, more important, the reader may interpret the passage in a way not intended by the writer.

Unless you are trying to create a special effect, remember that you must place a period (or question mark or exclamation point) after every simple, compound, or complex sentence. Anything less will result in a run-on sentence or a comma splice. It is not enough to argue that the reader can get the idea anyway, even if the punctuation is faulty. Sometimes he cannot. And always it is a bother to the reader when he is presented with a passage in which the sentence structure is poorly organized.

Here are two passages, the first written by a boy and the second by a young woman. Although both pieces of writing are interesting and rather charming, the first is weakened by too many unintentional run-on sentences, and the second is marred by frequent comma splices.

Yes because the husband goes out to work and earns all the money, most wives do the washing on Monday and the man comes home to dinner she's still hanging out the washing and there's no dinner waiting for him and he's got to fry himself some bacon and eggs for dinner and no man likes that and he gives her half his wages and hardly ever gets a square meal once a week. On Tuesday most wives go to Cambridge to buy a new hat or a skirt when he comes home he finds a note saying back by 8:00 gone Cambridge buy new hat dinner in the oven custard under grill. They only do housework and they have all the afternoon off because they have finished by dinner time.

From *Children's Writing,* by David Holbrook

One fine morning I got up, and went to bring the milk in to make some coffee, but at my disaster I found a young baby lying in a basket fast asleep, so I grabbed it quick and brought it in, it was a baby boy with light hair and blue eyes, well of course I would have loved to keep the child but I knew that wouldn't be right, so I telephoned the police, and told them everything that had happened, and told me to take the baby down to the police station. So I got ready and set off to the station. Of course I liked the baby and didn't want to give it to the police. They said that they would put up notices about the baby. They let me look after him until someone owned up.

A month later.

A month went but nobody owned up and the police were tired of looking everywhere for the parents that they said I could adopt the baby if I wanted to, if not they would put it in a home. I soon got married and talked it over with my husband, and he said it was OK, with him so, in a few day's time the baby was ours and weren't we pleased. So we all lived happily ever after.

From *English for the Rejected,* by David Holbrook

144

Obviously, the writers knew what they intended to say and knew in their minds where the sentences probably should end. But since they have failed to reproduce properly on paper the sentences in their minds, the reader must spend a great deal of unnecessary time deciphering and sometimes guessing at the writers' unexpressed or incorrectly expressed intentions. If you were puzzled by the young writers' opinions in the preceding passages, how much of your reaction was caused by the need to read their awkward styles with more than normal concentration?

activity

The following are examples of the run-on sentence and the comma splice. Rewrite each example with whatever sentence structures you think will convey the meaning clearly. Add punctuation and conjunctions as you need to. Afterward, compare your rewritten paragraphs with others in the class to see the different acceptable structures.

1 A few storm clouds gathered in the sky and we didn't notice them we were having so much fun with our volleyball game and at the first clap of thunder the rain came down so heavily we had to run to get under cover.

2 Pam wasn't sure whether to go to the rock concert, her friends urged her to go, she wanted to hear the music, but she was afraid of feeling trapped in the huge crowd, she arrived there and she was surprised, the music somehow made her feel happy to be with so many people.

3 I was walking in a daydream and suddenly I heard a loud clank of metal and shatter of glass and then people dashed out of buildings and I couldn't even see whether anyone was hurt, then I thought of my little brother playing on this block and I was frozen to the spot, finally the police moved the crowd back and no one was hurt at last I could move again.

4 Mark was already late for his dentist appointment when a friend stopped to tell him that the jacket he liked so much had just gone on sale he wasn't sure what to do since the sale was only for one day, he wanted to go to the store immediately if he missed this appointment, however, he wouldn't be able to get another one for a month despite his excitement about the jacket his toothache made the decision for him.

5 Courage is a quality that is not easily acquired, it cannot live only in the mind but must be practiced to be real, it can appear all at once when a situation calls for it, or it can be developed painstakingly over a long period of time, sometimes the reward of courage is public glory, but at other times its reward is known only to the one who has it.

145

COMMON PROBLEMS WITH COMPLEX SENTENCES

As we saw in the first section, the inserting process places one sentence inside another. Normally the insert sentence cannot stand alone without the main sentence into which it has been inserted. Although it cannot stand alone, the insert sentence is not any less important than the main sentence which receives it.

Read the following passage. All of the insert sentences have been removed from the original and are listed after the passage according to their numbered position. Read the reduced version without the inserts first; then read the passage with the inserts replaced. What effect is created in the complete version which is lacking in the reduced version? What kinds of effects are created by the insert sentences?

There was a shovel stuck in the snow. He picked it up, slung it over his shoulder and took off. He ran among the men and women   1   . Farther away, much farther, he stopped. He began to clear the sidewalk   2   . The snow wasn't muddy here. It was a white powder   3   The children could eat it or hide in it. But Philibert didn't see any children. The snow had a smell   4   . It was the smell of ashes.
    5   , he would then ask for what he had coming to him and go and find something to eat. There was a strength in his arms   6   Each shovelful of snow   7   was as important as one of his heartbeats.
    Then at last the path was cleared. The sidewalk looked nicely grey at the bottom of the trench   8
    He hesitated before the big oak door. But he was hungry.
    A light was turned on behind the square of opaque glass. The door was opened partway. Philibert pushed. The round head of a little old man shone in the doorway.
    "Shovel your walk for a quarter," said Philibert and he held out his hand.
    "No beggars," came the reply in English.
    Philibert was pushed back by the heavy door. He hadn't understood a word   9
    "Vieux Christ!   10   it won't be me that buries you," said Philibert.
    With his shovel and his feet Philibert put back all the snow   11

From *Is It the Sun, Philibert?* by Roch Carrier

1 who were walking along with their heads in their scarves
2 that led up to one of the houses, heaving big shovelfuls of snow
3 where children could slide and roll and go to sleep
4 that was carried to his face by the wind
5 When he had finished digging the passage through the snow
6 that would never have come to him if his father had asked him for help
7 that he moved from the front of this house
8 that he had cut through the snow
9 that the old man had muttered
10 If you drop dead
11 that he had removed from the sidewalk

You noticed that the insert sentences could come in any one of three places—before, after or in the middle of the main sentence. There are two main problems that may arise with insert sentences. One, called the *dangling modifier*, usually occurs at the beginning, when the insert is placed before the main sentence. The other is the *trailing sentence fragment*, which usually appears after the main sentence. Study the following collage and explain what is wrong with these sentences. See if you can distinguish between dangling modifiers and trailing sentence fragments.

Calmly munching oats in her stall, Barbara finally discovered her favorite horse.

Everyone at the dance wore tuxedoes. Because it was a formal affair.

Paralyzed with stage-fright, the sympathetic audience of parents watched the young ballerina as she stood helpless at center stage.

Paul Henderson scored in the last minute of play. Winning the game for Canada.

DANGLING MODIFIERS

The common form of the dangling modifier is the *"ing" phrase*. An "ing" phrase is really a reduced form of an insert sentence. It is sometimes called a *participial phrase*, because it begins with the present participle of a verb (verb + *ing*) used as a modifier. Study the following example.

Introductory clause

When Al had finished his meal, he folded his napkin and slowly rose from the table.

"Ing" phrase

Having finished his meal, Al folded his napkin and slowly rose from the table.

Notice the difference between the two examples. How does the "ing" phrase differ from the introductory clause? Who is the subject of the phrase, "having finished his meal"? Now study the next example and tell what is wrong with it.

After turning on the shower, the hot water scalded me.

How should the sentence read? How can you make the introductory "ing" phrase refer to "I" rather than to "hot water"? If you wish to avoid the problem of dangling modifiers, always check this rule:

Introductory "ing" phrases always refer to the subject in the main sentence.

Compare the two following passages. Both a and b examples use introductory "ing" phrases, but one does it correctly and the other incorrectly. Study the difference.

a Shortly after my adventure with the highwayman, I came to a fork in the road. *Having just been badly frightened,* I sat down by the roadside to compose my nerves. *Before making any decision as to which road to take,* I fumbled nervously through my knapsack for my handy supply of rum. *Raising the flask to my still trembling lips,* I began to realize how badly my confidence was shaken.

b Shortly after my adventure with the highwayman, I came to a fork in the road. *Having just been badly frightened,* the roadside seemed like a good place for me to sit down in order to compose my nerves. *Before making any decisions as to which road to take,* my handy supply of rum seemed like a good idea. *Raising the flask to my still trembling lips,* the realization came to me of how badly my confidence had been shaken.

You may have to read version b a few times to see why the "ing" phrases are technically illogical. You do get the general idea of what the writer is intending to say in b, but a close reading will show you that all of the phrases refer to the wrong noun in the main sentence. Dangling modifiers are often hard to spot, particularly in your own writing, because you always know what you intend the phrase to refer to. Failure to make it refer to the intended noun often produces confusing or humorous results.

Explain why the writer of the caption for the following picture was fired by his newspaper editor.

Leaping like a flying squirrel from one rooftop to another, the daring stuntcar driver put his auto through a series of impossible maneuvers.

activities

1 Suppose you are a very clever criminal lawyer. By applying your technical knowledge of grammar, show how you could interpret the following accusations in such a way that your clients would have to go free from the charges brought against them for murder.

a *defendant:* me

Deliberately cutting the rope, my partner fell to his death as I stood by laughing.

b *defendant:* the wife

After gulping down the poisoned glass of sherry, the wife quietly watched as her husband slowly slumped to the richly carpeted living room floor.

c *defendant:* the partisans

After drawing the pin from the grenade and hurling it in a careful arch, the tank exploded in flames as the partisans dived for cover.

2 Explain why the following examples are unintentionally humorous. Correct the sentences by altering the position of the nouns in the main sentence in order to make sure that the "ing" phrase refers to the intended noun.

a Frantically waving with outstretched arms, the bus ignored the parcel-laden pedestrian as it sped by.

b Quietly drinking a milk shake at the bar, the baby elephant's entrance surprised the boy at the soda fountain.

c Kicking the football through the goal posts, the referee signaled the end of the game.

d Holding a baby in one hand and a gun in the other, the startled bank teller handed over all her cash to the female bank robber.

e Stepping onto the lunar surface for the first time in history, command control "chewed-out" the embarrassed astronaut for slipping on a banana peel.

3 On the principle that making errors intentionally helps a writer to become more conscious of the problem, write your own examples of dangling modifiers. Choose a suitable prize for the most humorous example in your class.

MISPLACED PARTS

In addition to the dangling modifier, there are other parts of a sentence which may be misplaced, such as prepositional or adverbial phrases. Whether or not you can name the kind of misplaced part, you will usually be able to find it from the meaning of the sentence. Try doing this quiz, which is an assortment of misplaced parts. Which ones are examples of dangling modifiers?

1 *To which question, asked by David Susskind of a panel of photographers, was one of them justified in answering, "She's a lousy photographer"?*
   a What do you think of Ingrid Bergman as a photographer?
   b As a photographer, what do you think of Ingrid Bergman?

2 *In which sentence was the baseball battered?*
   a In the second inning the pitcher sustained a gash on the chin from a batted ball that required six stitches.
   b In the second inning a batted ball hit the pitcher's chin, making a gash that required six stitches.

3 *Which bus belongs in Disneyland?*
   a Hopping from one tired foot to the other, the crosstown bus finally came into view.
   b Hopping from one tired foot to the other, I finally saw the crosstown bus come into view.

4 *Which persons valued their lives cheaply?*
   a The obituary column lists the names of persons who died recently for a nominal fee.
   b The obituary column for a nominal fee lists the names of persons who died recently.

5 *Which judge seems also to be a philanthropist?*
   a Having paid my parking fine, I was dismissed by the judge with a reprimand.
   b Having paid my parking fine, the judge dismissed me with a reprimand.

6 *Which is unfair to the local fire department?*
   a The blaze was put out before any damage was done by the local fire department.
   b The blaze was put out by the local fire department before any damage was done.

7 *Which arrangement would be a bother for the First Lady?*
   a Our guests are then taken to the famous Hotel Willow within walking distance of the White House, where rooms are provided for them.
   b Our guests are then taken to their rooms at the famous Hotel Willow within walking distance of the White House.

8 *Which boys should be studying Latin or Greek instead of bucking the line?*
   a Being made of fragile material, the boys on the football team are having a hard time keeping their jerseys intact.
   b Being made of fragile material, the jerseys worn by the boys on the football team are hard to keep intact.

TRAILING SENTENCE FRAGMENTS

When speaking spontaneously in public, we will often find ourselves making a statement which we then follow up with a brief explanation. This is a very common pattern. We want to get our main idea out first; once this is done, we can then follow up the main sentence with a related explanatory footnote.

1 For instance, we might say the following:

a The writer and his family emigrated to Canada,

and then, after a pause, add the related statement:

b because they were looking for a new start in a young country.

Is the second statement an independent sentence, or is it part of the first sentence?

2 Consider this example:

a Soon students began to congregate in front of the school,

to which we then add this elaboration:

b some on foot, others on bicycles, and still others in cars.

3 Again, here the speaker makes an opening statement in acceptable sentence form:

a The responsibilities of a babysitter are almost endless,

and adds to this a further explanatory remark:

b such as reading bedtime stories, stopping fights, and tucking sleepy children into bed.

There is nothing to prevent us from making each of these examples a set of two independent main sentences, such as the following:

The writer and his family emigrated to Canada. They were looking for a new start in a young country.

Soon students began to congregate in front of the school. Some were on foot, others were on bicycles, and still others were in cars.

The responsiblities of a babysitter are almost endless. For instance, she has to read bedtime stories, stop fights, and tuck sleepy children into bed.

Notice the changes that were made in 1b, 2b, and 3b in order to make them independent sentences. In all of the three original examples, the (b) element is a kind of afterthought added onto the end of the main statement. The three original examples had the following structure:

Main statement, Elaboration

1 a Main sentence,   b insert sentence
2 a Main sentence,   b verbless phrase
3 a Main sentence,   b "ing" phrase

As we already know, insert sentences cannot stand alone; neither can verbless phrases or "ing" phrases. How then must these elaborations be punctuated? Are they independent sentences or not?

Which of the following are correct in written prose?

4 a The writer and his family emigrated to Canada. Because they were looking for a new start in a young country.

4 b Soon students began to congregate in front of the school. Some on foot, others on bicycles, and still others in cars.

4 c The responsibilities of a babysitter are almost endless. Such as reading bedtime stories, stopping fights, and tucking sleepy children into bed.

5 a The writer and his family emigrated to Canada, because they were looking for a new start in a young country.

5 b Soon students began to congregate in front of the school, some on foot, others on bicycles, and still others in cars.

5 c The responsibilities of a babysitter are almost endless, such as reading bedtime stories, stopping fights, and tucking sleepy children into bed.

The potential problem, as we have seen, is that while the trailing sentence fragment can be suitable in conversation, it does not read very well in formal written prose. If trailing sentence fragments are a problem in your writing, you may avoid them by placing the elaboration at the beginning of the sentence. You will then come up with this pattern:

Elaboration, Main statement

6 a Because they were looking for a new start in a young country, the writer and his family emigrated to Canada.

6 b Soon students, some of them on foot, others on bicycles, and still others in cars, began to congregate in front of the school.

6 c Reading bedtime stories, stopping fights, and tucking sleepy children into bed are just some of the almost endless responsibilities of a babysitter.

CONCLUSION

Explain why the editor of this book might have rejected the following copy.

When writing formal prose on paper,. several problems often crop up for the student. Such as the ones just studied. Thinking that prose is like speech, certain difficulties may arise for the young, inexperienced writer. Speaking lends itself to a much looser kind of sentence structure. As does writing advertising copy. But when writing formal prose, mistakes of a rather ludicrous kind may be made by the student. Dangling modifiers (like the last one). Or trailing sentence fragments (like this one). When writing correctly and effectively, the errors of faulty sentence structure may be avoided. Careful revision will catch most of these mistakes. The few moments spent in rereading your compositions could save a lot of embarrassment later. It is time well spent. Your own and your readers'!

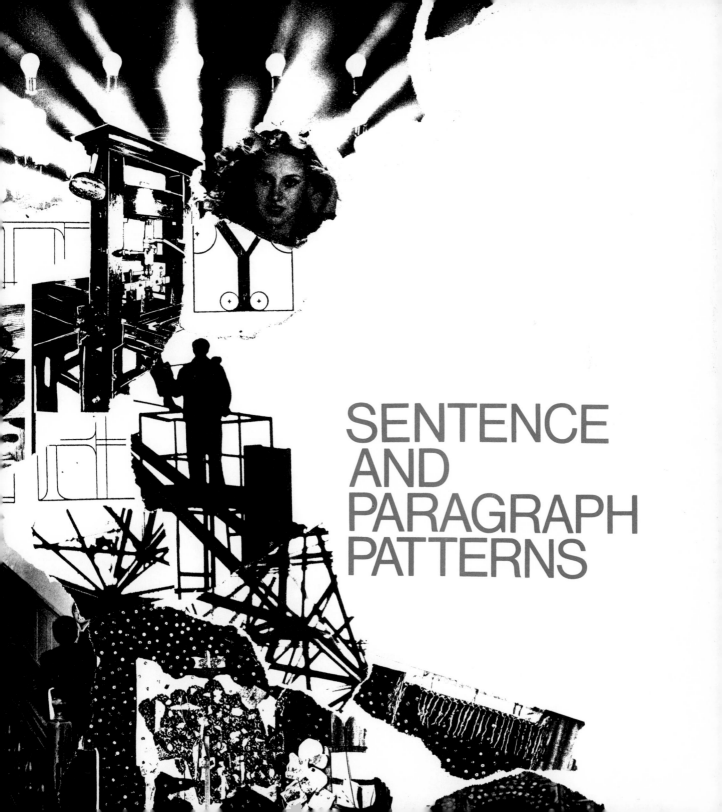

SENTENCE
AND
PARAGRAPH
PATTERNS

TEXTURE IN PAINTING AND WRITING

Painting with words on paper or with colors on canvas are two activities which have some things in common. Both the writer and the painter are interested in the creation of "pictures" which are vivid and appealing.

activity

Study the three versions of this picture. Notice how each successive version is richer in detail and texture. Now try to translate this scene into words in three stages. In stage one, use only simple sentences and little descriptive detail. In stage two, rewrite your first version by introducing only physical descriptive detail. In stage three, rewrite your second draft by adding emotional and atmospheric detail to the physical description.

By the gradual addition of vivid detail, a writer can paint a verbal image of rich texture. Look at the following excerpts of paragraphs from which most of the detail has been removed (a), and compare them with the complete versions (b).

2

1

3

a He listened to the hooting of many metal horns, the squealing of brakes, the calls of vendors. Colonel Freeleigh's feet began to move. His eyes squeezed tight. He gave a series of immense sniffs, as if to gain the odors of meats; the smell of stone alleys. He could feel the sun burn his spiny-bearded cheek, and he was twenty-five years old again.

b He listened to the hooting of many metal horns, the squealing of brakes, the calls of vendors *selling red-purple bananas and jungle oranges in their stalls.* Colonel Freeleigh's feet began to move, *hanging from the edge of his wheel chair, making the motions of a man walking.* His eyes squeezed tight. He gave a series of immense sniffs, as if to gain the odors of meats *hung on iron hooks in sunshine, cloaked with flies like a mantle of raisins;* the smell of stone alleys *wet with morning rain.* He could feel the sun burn his spiny-bearded cheek, and he was twenty-five years old again, *walking, walking, looking, smiling, happy to be alive, very much alert, drinking in colors and smells.*

a She was a woman with a broom or a dustpan or a washrag or a mixing spoon. You saw her cutting piecrust, or you saw her setting out the pies or taking them in. She rang porcelain cups. She glided through the halls as steadily as a vacuum machine. She made mirrors of every window. She strolled through any garden, and the flowers raised their quivering fires. She slept quietly and turned no more than three times in a night. Waking, she touched people like pictures.

b She was a woman with a broom or a dustpan or a washrag or a mixing spoon *in her hand.* You saw her cutting piecrust *in the morning, humming to it,* or you saw her setting out the *baked pies at noon* or taking them in, *cool, at dusk.* She rang porcelain cups *like a Swiss bell ringer, to their place.* She glided through the halls as steadily as a vacuum machine, *seeking, finding, and setting to rights.* She made mirrors of every window, *to catch the sun.* She strolled *but twice* through any graden, *trowel in hand,* and the flowers raised their quivering fires *upon the warm air in her wake.* She slept quietly and turned no more than three times in a night, *as relaxed as a white glove to which, at dawn, a brisk hand will return.* Waking, she touched people like pictures, *to set their frames straight.*

From *Dandelion Wine,* by Ray Bradbury

In what way does the "texture" of the second paragraph differ from that of the first paragraph? Is the detail included in b entirely physical, or does it do something else as well? What do you notice about *where* the extra detail in b occurs in each of the sentences? Can you give any reasons why the author might place this extra detail where he does?

The second version is obviously more richly detailed. Does this mean it is a better piece of writing? Certainly it is more effective, and the difference is mainly due to the inclusion of descriptive detail at the end of the main sentences. We will call these additional descriptive sections *terminal clusters*, because they come at the end of the main sentence. Not all descriptive and narrative writing employs terminal clusters, but it is a very common technique used by modern writers to give a passage greater richness in verbal texture.

SENTENCE COMBINING

THE TWO-LEVEL SENTENCE

Simple sentences may be combined in many ways to create quite different effects. As an example, consider the following two simple sentences:

Mary went into the drugstore.
She was dragging her doll behind her.

We can insert either one of these sentences inside the other. In either case, let us label the main sentence "level 1" and the insert, "level 2." We will begin with the pattern in which the insert comes first. This 2–1 pattern might look as follows:

2 When Mary went into the drugstore,
1 she was dragging her doll behind her.

or
2 Going into the drugstore,
1 Mary dragged her doll behind her.

The focus or emphasis in this 2–1 pattern is on the activity of Mary's dragging the doll. But we can reverse the process, giving us the following 1–2 pattern:

1 Mary went into the drugstore
2 dragging her doll behind her.

Notice how the feeling we get from the 1–2 pattern differs from that of the previous 2–1 pattern. The emphasis is different.

The 2–1 pattern focused at its conclusion upon what Mary was doing; she was dragging her doll. The 1–2 pattern focused first upon what Mary was doing and then added a descriptive detail to let us know something more about the way she was doing it. Thus, the emphasis in the structure of the 2–1 pattern leaves us with the more decisive effect of having learned a fact or reached a conclusion, whereas the 1–2 pattern leaves us with the more descriptive effect of having gained an additional atmospheric detail.

If we wrote the sentence as follows, we would lose much of the descriptive effect of the previous example sentence:

2 Dragging her doll behind her,
1 Mary went into the drugstore.

For expository writing the 2–1 pattern will often give the emphasis needed for a logical statement in which one fact follows from another. For descriptive purposes, the 1–2 pattern works well, because the descriptive tag at the end of a sentence acts as an effective postscript.

Compare, for instance, these alternate patterns:

Expository writing

2 When heated to 212 degrees Fahrenheit,
1 water changes from a liquid to a gas.

1 Water changes from a liquid to a gas,
2 when heated to 212 degrees Fahrenheit.

Descriptive writing

1 The water was boiling in the kettle,
2 whistling its merry kitchen tune.

2 Whistling its merry kitchen tune,
1 the water was boiling in the kettle.

The difference in effect between the two patterns for each sentence is a small one, yet there does seem to be a difference. Which pattern do you think sounds more appropriate for each example?

Modern writers seem to favor the 1–2 pattern for description and narration, partly because it creates a freer, more atmospheric effect. The 2–1 pattern is favored for certain types of expository writing where conclusive statements are important. Of course, these sentence patterns do not represent rules and restrictions for writing. They are meant only to help us see the way that sentence structure alters the effect of our verbal communication. There is meaning in the form as well as content of a sentence, and one way that we work with form is in the variations of the two-level sentence.

activities

1 Study the following passage from Margaret Laurence's novel, *The Stone Angel*. In the scene, an elderly lady is describing two children at play on a beach. Why is the sentence structure appropriate to the subject? Why does the writer occasionally use terminal clusters at level 2? How do the sentences in the 1–2 pattern differ from the single-level sentences? How does the author's sentence structure capture the impression of an old lady's dozing thoughts as she idly observes this simple scene?

1 A short distance along the beach two children are playing.
1 They've not seen me.
1 They're absorbed,
  2 deeply concentrating.

1 A boy and a girl,
  2 both around six, I'd say.
1 The boy has straight black hair.
1 The girl's hair is light brown and long,
  2 bunched into an elastic at the back of her head.
1 They're playing house—
  2 that much is obvious.
1 The boy is searching for clam shells.
1 He trots along the sand,
  2 head down, peering, stooping to pick one up here and there.
1 He rinses them in the water,
  2 paddling in a short way in his bare feet
1 and then returns.

2 Compare the two following versions of a passage from Rachel Carson's *The Edge of the Sea*. The only difference between the two is the sentence structure. In which is the rhythm more expository? In which does it sound more descriptive and poetic? Because the book from which the passage was taken is about ecology, which version do you think would be more appropriate to the subject matter? Which version do you prefer? Pick out examples of the 1–2 pattern in version b. Is the author interested in telling us something about ecology or in painting a vivid picture for us to imagine? Which version is more richly "textured"?

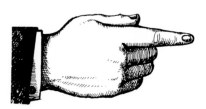

a In quieter waters, the seaweeds dominate the shore. They occupy every inch of space that the conditions of the tidal rise and fall allow them. By the sheer force of abundant and luxuriant growth, they force other shore inhabitants to accommodate to their pattern.

Above the high-tide line there is little change. On the shores of bays and estuaries, the microplants blacken the rocks. The lichens come down. They tentatively approach the sea . . . But on sheltered coasts the whole band of shore (the shore is marked out by the tides of the moon's quarters) is occupied by a swaying submarine forest. The forest is sensitive to the movements of the waves and the tidal currents. The trees of the forest are the large seaweeds. They are known as the rockweeds or sea wracks. They are stout of form and rubbery of texture. Here all other life exists within their shelter. The shelter is very hospitable to small things. They need protection from drying air, from rain, and from the surge of the running tides and the waves. The life of these shores is therefore incredibly abundant.

b In quieter waters, the seaweeds dominate the shore, occupying every inch of space that the conditions of tidal rise and fall allow them and by the sheer force of abundant and luxuriant growth forcing other shore inhabitants to accommodate to their pattern.

Above the high-tide line there is little change, and on the shores of bays and estuaries, the microplants blacken the rocks and the lichens come down and tentatively approach the sea . . . But on sheltered coasts the whole band of shore marked out by the tides of the moon's quarters is occupied by a swaying submarine forest, sensitive to the movements of the waves and the tidal currents. The trees of the forest are the large seaweeds known as the rockweeds or sea wracks, stout of form and rubbery of texture. Here all other life exists within their shelter—a shelter so hospitable to small things needing protection from drying air, from rain, and from the surge of the running tides and waves, that the life of these shores is incredibly abundant.

DIFFERENT STRUCTURES OF THE 1–2 PATTERN

In 1–2 pattern sentences, there are many different structures that can be used in level 2. In other words, terminal clusters can be put together in several ways.

It is easy to identify the different structures by looking at the type of word used as the head word in that cluster. Here are four examples of different terminal clusters; the head word in each cluster is italicized for you. By identifying the head word's part of speech, you can identify the structure of the whole cluster.

a
    1 He walked nervously into the center of the room
      2 *with* his hands stuffed deep inside his trouser pockets.

b
  1 Instinctively his right hand fingered his
    lucky charm,
     2 the *stone* he had found on the deserted
      beach.

c
  1 He looked up fearfully into the old man's
    face,
     2 *dark* and menacing in the dim light of
      the empty room.

d
  1 The skier flew down the treacherous
    course,
     2 *darting* madly between the slender
      flagpoles.

What is the part of speech of each of the head
words—*with, stone, dark* and *darting?* When you
have identified the part of speech of the head
word, you know that level 2 is either a *preposition cluster*, a *noun cluster*, an *adjective cluster*,
or a *verbal cluster.*

activity

Read the following brief paragraph:

The defenseman charged into the unsuspecting
forward. The forward fell with a crash into the
boards. A chorus of whistles went up from the
crowd.

Just how much descriptive power may be
gained by using terminal clusters can be seen by
studying this expanded version of the original
paragraph.

Hockey Night in Moscow

1 The defenseman charged into the unsuspecting forward
   2 *with* his arms and elbows high to deliver
    a vicious check.
1 The forward fell with a crash into the boards,
   2 his *head* hitting the ice with stunning force.
1 A chorus of whistles went up from the crowd,
   2 *angry* and *incensed* at the demonstration
    of rough play.

What difference in speed and pace did you
notice between the abbreviated and the
expanded versions? Does descriptive detail
always slow down the movement of a piece of
writing?

One of the most useful structures which can
add drama and excitement to a piece of writing
is the *verbal cluster.* Terminal verbal clusters
(sometimes called *participial phrases*) are very
important structures for narrative writing. Consider, for instance, this passage which is taken
from the end of William Golding's novel, *Lord of
the Flies.* The hero, Ralph, is desperately at-
tempting to avoid the crazed pursuit of Jock's
band of bloodlusting young boys.

He shot forward, burst the thicket, was in the
open *screaming* snarling bloody. He swung the
stake and the savage tumbled over; but there were
others *coming* towards him, *crying* out. He
swerved as a spear flew past, and then was silent,
running. At once the lights *flickering* ahead of
him merged together and a tall bush directly in
his path burst into a great fan-shaped flame. He
swung to the right, *running* desperately fast, with
the heat *beating* on his left side and the fire *racing*

forward like a tide. He forgot his wounds, his hunger and thirst became fear, hopeless fear on flying feet, *rushing* through the forest towards the open beach. He stumbled over a root and the cry that pursued him rose even higher. He saw a shelter burst into flames and the fire flapped at his right shoulder and there was the glitter of water. Then he was down, *rolling* over and over in the warm sand, *crouching* with arm up to ward off, *trying* to cry for mercy.

For the creation of action and excitement, the verbal tag (verb + *ing*) is obviously a very effective structure.

The device that most appeals to the imagination is the *simile cluster*. A simile is a comparison which begins with the word "like." The head word in a simile cluster, then, is the preposition "like," and the simile cluster is actually a particular type of prepositional cluster. Here are two examples:

1 The blackened figure staggered from the burning building
  2 *like* some dark devil emerging from the fires of hell.

1 Its mouth was open in a silent scream which punctuated the dark
  2 *like* a crazed exclamation mark.

Simile clusters help you to introduce comparisons of a highly imaginative kind to your writing. The simile cluster is frequently combined with the noun cluster to enrich its visual appeal or added to the verbal cluster to increase its speed or pace. Consider these examples:

1 The diver swung out over the face of the rocks,
  2 her *body* momentarily arched over the waves
    3 *like* a ballerina held aloft at the top of her lift.

1 He drove through the maze of players to the basket
  2 *leaping* high above the defenders' outstretched arms
    3 *like* a trampoline artist defying gravity.

When added to another cluster, the simile cluster creates an imaginative "piling on" of pictures. The techniques whereby a writer piles one effect on top of another will be investigated in the next section, which deals with the multi-level sentence.

activities

1 Identify the types of clusters used in the level 2 tags in the following prose passage. Does any type predominate?

Finney balanced at the end of the springboard *with* his arms outstretched in front of his tensed body. At the whistle, he jackknifed into the water, *cutting* the surface cleanly *like* a smooth torpedo. He surfaced quickly *like* a sounding porpoise, *arms* and legs already churning the beaten water of the pool. His feet fluttered delicately, *driven* by the twin pistons of his powerful thighs. His arms moved relentlessly in and out of the water, *arms* that rose and fell with the regularity of a turning windmill. At each backstroke his hands swept a spray of water behind him, the *fingers* cupped *like* two small scoops for maximum power. At each double stroke his head twisted backwards, *mouth* gaping as it sucked in air from the hollow formed by the wake of his prowlike head as it cut through the water. Once, twice, three times he swam the double length of the pool, *oblivious* to the cries of encouragement from his teammates, *eyes* focused solely on the approaching finish line. And then he was there *exhausted* in every fiber of his muscular young body. He relaxed in the water *waiting* calmly for the official result *with* his head bobbing listlessly in the tiny wavelets.

2 Combine each of the following pairs of sentences in such a way that the second sentence becomes a level 2 descriptive tag (or terminal cluster). The head word in the second sentence is italicized and should become the head word of your noun, adjective, verbal, preposition, or simile cluster. You may have to omit some words and change the form of others. Here is an example which is done for you.

The humpback whale rose from the ocean depths. It *spewed* from its blowhole a giant column of water.

The humpback whale rose from the ocean depths, *spewing* from its blowhole a giant column of water.

a The truck roared down the deserted highway. Its *headlights* stabbed the darkness like two arcing searchlights.

b When Alice returned home from the party, she was crying. She was *unhappy* and ashamed that no one had asked her to dance, or even spoken to her.

c The crowd of visitors lined up for a glimpse of Dr. Kissinger. They were *like* children waiting in line to visit Santa Claus.

d The fullback crashed over the center of the line. He was moving *with* legs churning and body twisting in a desperate attempt at a last minute score.

3 Complete the following sentences by composing your own original simile clusters. Try for unusual and imaginative comparisons.

a The day dribbled on so slowly, and the evening like . . .
b His hair was long and tangled and greasy, and hung down, and you could see his eyes shining through like . . .
c Dawn began not as a gorgeous fanfare over the ocean as I had expected, but as a strange gray thing, like . . .
d In the dawn the harbor was bleak and steel-colored, extending into the whitened land like . . .
e He beat his foot upon the ground and scowled with hate at the swirling smoke that was approaching like . . .
f Her presence in the house seemed to him a most lovely and disturbing thing, like . . .

As you have probably guessed by now, the partial sentences above are fragments of sentences written by professional authors. You can compare your creations with the originals by turning to the completions on page 166.

THE MULTI-LEVEL SENTENCE

As we found in the last section, when painting with words or with color, the writer or the artist may often be doing similar things. Consider the two works of art on the following pages.

One is a silk screen picture by Andy Warhol of a woman. In it the same portrait is repeated twenty times, each with a slightly different background color. The other picture is Michelangelo's famous painting of the creation of Adam, itself only a part of the enormous mural on the ceiling of the Sistine Chapel. Both pictures are descriptive, but there are many differences in the approaches to the subjects.

Two principles which are used as much in writing as in painting are *repetition* and *movement*. As an example, read this sentence which might be suggested by the Andy Warhol picture.

1 The New York society woman is an almost invisible person,

2 dressed anonymously in a "basic black" dress that might put her working sisters six months in the red,

2 careful that her hair and makeup do not show the secret hours of elaborate preparation,

2 chauffeured unseen through crowds in her luxurious limousine from one good work to another,

2 everywhere unrecognized except by those little luxuries that make life itself endurable.

If you compare the written with the visual portrait, it should be easier to see the parallel between the structure of the sentence and the structure of the painting.

164

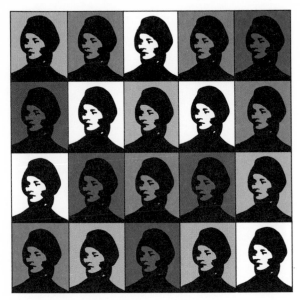

1 The New York society woman is an almost invisible person,

2 careful that her hair and makeup do not show the secret hours of elaborate preparation,

2 chauffeured unseen through crowds in her luxurious limousine from one good work to another,

2 dressed anonymously in a "basic black" dress that might put her working sisters six months in the red,

2 everywhere unrecognized except by those little luxuries that make life itself endurable.

1 What words in each of the descriptive tags reinforce the idea that this type of woman is "an almost invisible person"?

2 What did you notice about the structure of all of the descriptive tags?

3 Although each successive descriptive tag adds new detail, how do they all focus back on the same subject?

4 Why is the repetitive structure appropriate to the topic of the whole sentence?

5 In what way is the repetitive structure of the sentence similar to the repetitive organization of the picture? How are they different?

Now consider this sentence, which was suggested by Michelangelo's painting shown on the following pages.

Answers from page 163.

a like sand through an egg-timer. (*The Stone Angel*, Margaret Laurence)

b like he was behind vines. (*Huckleberry Finn*, Mark Twain)

c like sunshine seen through burlap. (*A Separate Peace*, John Knowles)

d like a scimitar with broken edges, stained by fragments of debris drifting with the tide. (*Barometer Rising*, Hugh MacLennan)

e like a phantom flood. (*The Red Badge of Courage*, Stephen Crane)

f like a sudden strain of music. (*Jalna*, Mazo de la Roche)

1 From the finger of God to the hand of Adam, the flow of life suddenly darts

2 like a brilliant spark jumping between two electrodes,

3 the current running up the curve of Adam's outstretched arm and

4 exploding beneath his flickering eyelids

5 with the power and vision of wakening delight.

1 From the finger of God to the hand of Adam, the flow of life suddenly darts

2 like a brilliant spark jumping between two electrodes,

3 the current running up the curve of Adam's outstretched arm and

4 exploding beneath his flickering eyelids

5 with the power and vision of
   wakening delight.

1 Where does the focus of the eye move in the painting? How does the sentence also capture some of this movement? List the words that show how the attention moves from one detail to another in the whole sentence.

2 In what way is this painting and sentence more dramatic than the previous pair?

3 What do you notice about the structure of each of the descriptive tags? Are they similar to each other?

4 Why would a repetitive structure be less appropriate to the subject of the creation of Adam?

5 Underline the head word in each of the four descriptive tags. What do you notice about the four parts of speech? What type is each of the descriptive tags?

The two sentences which we have just observed are examples of multi-level sentences. In each, a main clause is followed by two, three, or four descriptive tags. But in addition, we have seen that the structure of the descriptive tags in the multi-level sentence can be arranged in two different patterns.

One pattern presents a string of descriptive tags which all have the same basic structure. The pattern is repeated in such a way that each tag parallels the structure of the preceding tag or tags. This general arrangement is called the pattern of *parallel repetition*.

The second pattern is quite different. Each tag is different in structure from the one preceding or following it, yet each is linked in some way to the one going before. The effect created is something like the links in a chain, and for this reason the general organization is described by the term *chain linking*.

We have seen how these two patterns— parallel repetition and chain linking—can be used as well in the structure and organization of a picture as in writing. Now let us see the particular strengths or advantages of each pattern. Which pattern is more appropriate for the purpose of dramatic emphasis, and which is more useful for the creation of dramatic movement? Consider first this outline of the two patterns:

Parallel repetition	*Chain linking*
1 Main clause	1 Main clause
2 Cluster A	2 Cluster A
2 Cluster A	3 Cluster B
2 Cluster A	4 Cluster C

In parallel repetition, all the clusters have the same grammatical structure. Notice that in the chain linking pattern, each cluster has a different grammatical structure: verbal, noun, adjective, preposition or simile cluster.

The diagram may be simplified even further. The number 1 is used for the main clause, which usually comes at the beginning of the whole sentence. The tags following it are all numbered the same if their structure is the same, or given different numbers if their structures are different.

Parallel repetition   *Chain linking*

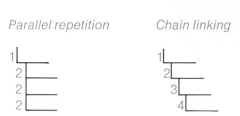

We can now look at some examples and study the different effects that each of these patterns creates. First of all, consider this sentence. Which pattern does it illustrate?

1 Hetty's constantly moving hands seemed to have a life of their own,
  2 *clutching* at the air about her lap,
  2 *plucking* nervously at the rough fabric of her skirt, and
  2 *squeezing* themselves white around the edges of her wooden chair.

The sentence can be easily diagrammed in the following way:

1 | Main clause
  2 | Verbal cluster
  2 | Verbal cluster
  2 | Verbal cluster

The grammatical structure of each of the tags is the same: all of them are verbal clusters. Repetition is used to focus the reader's attention on the activity of Hetty's hands. From this detail, we can infer something about Hetty's general emotional state.

The pattern of parallel repetition is an effective technique for the creation of emphasis. All of our attention is focused on the movement of Hetty's hands to the exclusion of everything else. Parallel repetition, then, sacrifices something of the overall picture to focus more closely on one specific point of emphasis.

The pattern of chain linking is quite different in the effect it creates. Consider this example:

1 A variety of small gestures betrayed Hetty's growing nervousness:
  2 *fearful* and *desperate* in tiny ways, she stood
    3 *looking* furtively at the ticking clock
      4 *like* a child waiting for recess to rescue her from the nameless terrors of the classroom,
        5 *with* her hands plucking surreptitiously at her woolen skirt and her fingers whitening at the knuckles.

The different structures in the various terminal tags can be diagrammed as follows:

1 | Main clause
  2 | Adjective cluster
    3 | Verbal cluster
      4 | Simile cluster
        5 | Preposition cluster

Looking at the sentence, you will notice that it tends to move in a particular way. It starts with a general description of Hetty's emotions and moves progressively to more and more specific detail, ending with a tight focus on her hands and fingers.

Most of the time, the chain linking pattern develops in this way, moving from the general to the specific. It is something like a motion picture technique in which the camera moves from a wide to a tight focus. The advantage of chain linking, then, is in creating dramatic movement. It moves or varies emphasis within the overall picture.

You are given groups of sentences below and asked to combine each group into a single multi-level sentence. The head word is italicized to help you decide whether to use the pattern of parallel repetition or of chain linking. In reducing the secondary sentences to clusters, you may have to omit or change the form of various words. Be prepared to tell which pattern you have used. An example is done for you.

The chimpanzee swung noisily into the tree. Its *hair* stood on end. It looked *like* a porcupine bristling with fear.

1 The chimpanzee swung noisily into the tree,
  2 its *hair* standing on end
    3 *like* a porcupine bristling with fear.

    Pattern: chain linking

a He stood all alone in the middle of the empty bus depot. He had *his hat* in his hand. He carried *his hopes* in his suitcase and *his heart* in his mouth.

b He pulled off his glasses and gently rubbed his tired eyes. He had *eyes* that had lost themselves in the finer print of legal lore. He had *eyes* that in searching for truth had never seen it in himself or in a flower. He had *eyes* that were forever blind.

c They shot down the rapids in their tiny canoe. The *waters* foamed in fury all around them. They *held* their now useless paddles above their heads in a vain gesture. They seemed *like* lost children praying to a merciless river god.

d When the moon rose silently, it shone palely down on a scene of terrible carnage. *Men* writhed slowly in speechless agony. They moved *with* bodies twisted grotesquely. They were *like* statues broken and fallen around an ancient altar of heathen sacrifice.

We have been contrasting parallel repetition and chain linking as if the two patterns existed in complete independence of each other. In actual practice, writers often tend to mix the two patterns together in many different combinations. The mixed multi-level sentence draws upon the strength of both parallel repetition and chain linking patterns. When used appropriately, the mixture of both patterns can be highly effective.

Consider this example taken from a short story by Alden Nowlan:

1 She could remember
  2 how he'd walked with that easy slouch,
    3 his arms not swinging much,
    3 hands never moving far from his hips,
      4 stooping a little,
    3 his eyes half shut, and
  2 how he'd drawled,
      4 wrinkling his nose,
      4 making his voice sound more casual and throaty than usual when he got angry.

It would be rather difficult to judge which pattern predominates in this sentence. And yet both patterns work together in a very subtle way — chain linking to provide variety and dynamic movement, and parallel repetition to create emphasis and tight focus. The skillful writer can use these two simple patterns in many different combinations in order to create effects of startling variety.

activities

1 In the following examples each sentence is written in the chain linking pattern. On a sheet of paper, add a cluster in the position shown by the line, which is in parallel construction to the cluster immediately preceding it. The addition will change the original version into a mixed multi-level sentence. An example is done for you.

1 The tiny Indian village was deep in spring mud
  2 with children playing merrily in the pools of water,
    3 oblivious to the swarming clouds of black flies and
    3 _____

1 The tiny Indian village was deep in spring mud
  2 with children playing merrily in the pools of water,
    3 oblivious to the swarming clouds of black flies and
    3 happy in the promise of summer's short bloom.

a 1 The motorcycle tore up the steep dirt track,
   2 with wheels spinning wildly in the slippery mud
   2 with_____
     3 like an aimless meteor bent on self-destruction.

b 1 The lightning split the twisted old tree down the middle
   2 like an axe chopping through dry kindling,
    3 striking sparks in the dry undergrowth and
    3 _____

c 1 The children, victims of war, stood listlessly around the empty pot,
   2 too tired to protest their neglect,
    3 with bellies bloated by famine and
    3 with_____

d 1 The awesome avalanche rolled down the mountain slope
   2 like a white fist punching through tissue paper,
      3 snapping giant trees like matchsticks, and
      3 _____

e 1 The ominous black cloud approached at impossible speeds
   2 hurtling through space on a direct collision course with planet Earth,
   2 _____
      3 its size increasing hourly in the darkening sky above.

2 Study the picture on the opposite page. Write a mixed multi-level sentence that captures some of the action that is going on in it. Compare your sentence with others in the class.

3 Divide your class into three groups. Have each group take one of the following multi-level sentences and see if it falls into the pattern of parallel repetition, chain linking, or a mixture of the two.

a It was a handsome day, one of those clear, breezy spring mornings when the sky is a blue well, without a bottom, with now-and-then puff-ball clouds floating in it like blossoms off a snowball bush.

From *The Travels of Jaimie McPheeters,* by Robert Lewis Taylor

b They charged, hurling their bodies against the barrel, trying to break through the barrier, knocking it over, rolling it to its side and scrambling for a position at the opening.

From *Rabbit Boss,* by Thomas Sanchez

c During the day he would not think of it, and when it would come to him, when he would least expect it, he would turn his face to the sun, his eyes open, and the brilliance of the mountain light would drive the memory of the dream back, pushing it deep in his mind, flooding it with light, drowning it in whiteness.

From *Rabbit Boss,* by Thomas Sanchez

PATTERNS IN PARAGRAPH ORGANIZATION

In chapter 5, the sentence was defined as "a string of words that fall into natural groups." Just as a sentence is made up of a string of words, a paragraph is made up of a string of sentences. But do the sentences in a paragraph fall into natural groups in the way that words in a sentence do? Does a paragraph have any internal structure? What holds it together? What makes a paragraph complete? How many sentences might there be in a paragraph?

Look first at the pictures on the opposite page. How could they be used to make a point or to tell a story? Obviously the same pictures could be used for different purposes, but something will be needed in each case. We must have a focus, an idea to center the pictures upon. Here is one possibility:

a

1 Benjamin was one of those bright, handsome, no-nonsense cats that you find only once in a lifetime.

2 He was never a fighter, but other animals seemed to make way for him.

2 He was a great adventurer, and nothing thrilled him more than a ride in the car.

2 He could outrun any animal in the neighborhood, although stalking gave him more satisfaction.

2 He was as regal as a lion, but he also knew when to be gentle.

Again, we can take the same pictures and give them a different focus:

b

1 The first day we moved to the farm, I knew that our cat approved.

2 Benjamin's adventures began with a visit to the goats.

3 After inspecting their food, he discovered there was a new truck that would take him out to bigger fields.

4 Running through the grasses, he found new smells and sounds.

5 That evening, he greeted all of us happily and headed straight for his food.

6 He had never seemed so thoroughly content.

These paragraphs illustrate a number of things. First is the idea of *focus*. The focus of a paragraph is the key point, the main idea. In the same way that a camera brings a picture into focus, the sentences in a paragraph focus on an idea to make it clear.

The sentence that focuses most sharply on the idea is called the *topic sentence*. Often, though not always, the topic sentence appears at the beginning of a paragraph. The remaining sentences are usually organized in one of two basic patterns. Once the topic sentence has focused on an idea, the other sentences emphasize and support or move and develop it.

What are the topic sentences of the two example paragraphs, a and b? Now look at the structure of the rest of each paragraph. In what way are these two paragraphs similar to the two patterns we have already found in multi-level sentences? We can easily diagram the organizations of the two examples to show that one is parallel repetition and the other, a chain linking structure.

a
1 Topic sentence
2 _____
2 _____
2 _____

b
1 Topic sentence
2 _____
3 _____
4 _____

We learned in the discussion of multi-level sentences that the structure of parallel repetition emphasizes the main idea. In what different ways might you want to use emphasis in a paragraph? Suppose that you were asked on a history test to tell in one paragraph the conditions in this country just after the Civil War. You might write something like this:

At the end of the Civil War, the country was in a state of turmoil. There was bitterness in both the North and the South because of the bloodshed of the war. Thousands of newly freed, homeless ex-slaves were wandering about the land. Many cities and railroads lay in a state of ruin. Much of the currency afloat had become worthless.

Here parallel repetition appears in expository writing as a series of supporting examples. Notice that the topic sentence has been placed at the beginning. The sentences following it are a series, each of which emphasizes the main idea.

The supporting sentences all function in a parallel way in the paragraph; they are not absolutely linked to one another. In other words, the order of the last four sentences could be changed, or a sentence could be taken away, without destroying the sense of the paragraph. We can see, then, that either a series of examples or a description of events happening at the same time can make good use of the pattern of parallel repetition.

Now return to the Civil War paragraph for a moment. Can the topic sentence be placed somewhere else in it? Try rewriting the paragraph, changing as few words as possible, with the topic sentence at the end. Is the pattern still parallel repetition?

Here is another example of a parallel structure, this time in a descriptive paragraph. Notice how the entire paragraph focuses on the idea of "quiet, patient folk":

Still-fishermen are generally quiet, patient folk with a touch of poetry in their souls. They seldom talk about it, but they find something soothing and reassuring in a river bank or a pond, at dawn, at dusk, even at midday when the fish seldom bite. They know the quiet waters, these fishermen, and the look of a mud turtle on a log, the quick beat of a kingfisher's wings, the flash of a dragonfly. They know sunrise and sunset. They know where a man can have an hour's meditation between bites as well as where he can be kept so busy he has no time for thought or worry.

From *This Hill, This Valley,* by Hal Borland

Here the parallel structure was used to make the description fuller and more moving.

While a paragraph structured in parallel repetition is held together by the common emphasis of each sentence, a paragraph built with chain linking is held together by the development or movement of an idea. As before, the topic sentence provides a focus, but the remaining sentences move in a sequence through time or through a line of thought. Look, for example, at this paragraph:

Clarence "Bob" Birdseye, the Father of Frozen Food, was often heard to remark that the credit for quick-freezing should go to the Eskimos, who had been using it for centuries. And we know that in 1626 Francis Bacon was mulling over the idea of preserving flesh by freezing one snowy day as he rode from London to Highgate. Deciding to test his theory then and there, Bacon stopped at a cottage and bought a fowl, killed it and stuffed the carcass with snow. The poor man recorded that the experiment was a success, but he died shortly thereafter from the exposure he had suffered during it. Whoever his predecessors were, however, it was Birdseye who first succeeded in the practical freezing of food on a commercial scale.

From *Why Did They Name It . . . ?* by Hannah Campbell

If you try to change the order of the sentences in this paragraph or to remove any of them, the meaning will be lost. Each idea or event moves into the next one, while all of them move into the main idea. What is the topic sentence of this paragraph? Why would a chain-linking structure be suitable for narrative writing or for argumentation?

Now that we know the structural patterns that a paragraph can take, we still need to find out when a paragraph is complete. How many sentences should be in a paragraph? The answer to this question—like the discussion earlier in this book on complete sentences—can change according to the communication situation. Look again for a moment at the ad on page 123 and the questions following it. In advertising and in some journalism and fiction, the one-sentence paragraph appears for special emphasis. In more formal fiction and expository writing, however, paragraphs of at least two sentences are expected.

When trying to decide where to paragraph your writing, it is helpful to think of a new paragraph as a change of focus, a change of idea, or a change of time. Look back to the paragraph on conditions after the Civil War. In a longer essay, each one of the sentences in that paragraph could be the topic sentence for a new paragraph. Each new paragraph, then, would focus on a different point in greater detail, while all of the paragraphs would relate to the post-Civil War period.

Suppose, however, that your topic extended over a greater period of time than only immediately following the Civil War. You might then decide to start a new paragraph because of a change in time. You might continue with:

It was not long before Congress realized that a plan was needed to reunite the country. The plan that was enacted is referred to today as Reconstruction.

Notice that the phrase, "It was not long before," signals a change of time or a change of focus. A new paragraph structure has been set up for the discussion of Reconstruction. Transition words and phrases such as "however," "in any case," "suddenly," or "nevertheless" can be signals for the start of a new paragraph, although it is wise to avoid cluttering your writing with too many transitions of this kind.

It is not quite as easy to decide where to end a paragraph as it is to tell where to end a sentence, for the simple reason that we do not hear or think in paragraphs as we can do in sentences. If in your writing, however, each paragraph has a clear focus expressed in a topic sentence, you should have little trouble detecting a shift of focus which signals a new paragraph.

As we discovered in our study of multi-level sentences, the patterns of parallel repetition and chain linking are more likely to be found in combination with each other than completely alone. The advantage of this mixture is that the writer can draw on the strengths of both processes in the same paragraph. Chain linking provides an opportunity for the development of a line of thought or argument, while parallel repetition allows for the creation of certain types of emphasis.

Consider, for example, this brief selection from a historic speech by Martin Luther King addressed in August 28, 1963, to a large crowd of civil rights demonstrators before the Lincoln Memorial in Washington. Notice how the speaker swings from the chain linking pattern at the beginning to parallel repetition at the end. What is the reason for positioning the repetition at the end?

Five score years ago, a great American in whose symbolic shadow we stand today signed the Emancipation Proclamation. This momentous decree was a great beacon light of hope to millions of Negro slaves who had been seared in the flames of withering injustice. It came as a joyous daybreak to end the long night of their captivity. But one hundred years later, the Negro still is not free. One hundred years later, the life of the Negro is still badly crippled by the manacles of segregation and the chains of discrimination. One hundred years later, the Negro lives on a lonely island of poverty in the midst of a vast ocean of material prosperity. One hundred years later, the Negro still languishes in the corners of American society and finds himself in exile in his own land. So, we've come here today to dramatize a shameful condition.

If we diagram the key phrases of the paragraph, we can notice the way in which the speaker uses "echo words" at the beginning to connect his sentences in a chain linking fashion.

1 Five score years ago; Emancipation Proclamation
  2 This decree; beacon light
    3 joyous daybreak
      4 One hundred years later
      4 One hundred years later
      4 One hundred years later
      4 One hundred years later
        5 a shameful condition

Throughout the address, Martin Luther King relies very heavily on rhetorical repetition. The reason for this is twofold. First, he is drawing on the tradition of pulpit oratory, in which repetition is a very important rhetorical device. Second, in speeches of any kind, repetition tends to be used more heavily than in writing. The reason for this fact is that we tend to process information less efficiently through our ears than through our eyes. Because we cannot go back to check out some point we may have missed while listening to a speaker, the speaker must be careful to repeat his key ideas frequently enough to sink into the minds of his audience. Then too, if used correctly, repetition has a way of stirring the listeners' emotions and passions in a very powerful way. It is, therefore, a persuasive device which all great speakers tend to rely on rather heavily.

activities

1 Reread the excerpt from Martin Luther King's speech on page 178. Make a collage which visually illustrates some of the ideas and images mentioned in the eight-sentence passage. Is there any visual way to represent the verbal structure of parallel repetition?

2 Read the following passage from Winston Churchill's great speech to the British people on June 4, 1940. This speech was broadcast at one of the darkest moments of the Second World War, just following the defeat of France by the Germans and the withdrawal of the British Expeditionary Force at Dunkirk. Study the sentence structure to see how Churchill made use of chain linking and parallel repetition. Which structure best shows the sense of stubborn determination and valiant strength that we commonly associate with this great statesman and leader of the British people?

I have full confidence that if all do their duty, if nothing is neglected, we shall prove ourselves once again able to defend our island home, to ride out the storm of war, and to outlive the menace of tyranny, if necessary for years, if necessary alone. Even though large tracts of Europe and many old and famous states have fallen or may fall into the grip of the Gestapo and all the odious apparatus of Nazi rule, we shall not flag or fail. We shall go on to the end. We shall fight in France. We shall fight on the seas and oceans. We shall fight with growing confidence and growing strength in the air. We shall defend our island whatever the costs may be. We shall fight on the beaches. We shall fight on the landing grounds. We shall fight in the field and in the streets. We shall fight in the hills. We shall never surrender, and even if, which I do not for a moment believe, this island or a large part of it were subjugated or starving, then our Empire beyond the seas, armed and guarded by the British fleet, would carry on the struggle, until, in God's good time, the New World, with all its power and might, steps forth to the rescue and liberation of the old.

3 Compare Snoopy's use of parallel repetition on the following page with Charles Dickens' use of repetition in the first sentence of his novel, *A Tale of Two Cities:*

It was the best of times, it was the worst of times, it was the age of wisdom, it was the age of foolishness, it was the epoch of belief, it was the epoch of incredulity, it was the season of Light, it was the season of Darkness, it was the spring of hope, it was the winter of despair, we had everything before us, we had nothing before us, we were all going direct to Heaven, we were all going direct the other way—in short, the period was so far like the present period, that some of its noisiest authorities insisted on its being received, for good or for evil, in the superlative degree of comparison only.

CONCLUSION

If a piece of writing is to be vivid and imaginative, it should have detail that creates texture, as in a painting.

1 We began our study of "texture" by reviewing the various patterns in the two-level sentence,
  2 the main clause followed by various types of terminal clusters.
1 We built from the two-level sentence to the multi-level sentence
  2 with its two patterns of parallel repetition and chain linking,
    3 studying the strengths of each pattern separately and
    3 noting the ways in which both patterns can be mixed together.
1 Finally, we moved from the organization of sentences to the structure of the whole paragraph.
  2 We observed that paragraphs can be based on the same two patterns that are used in multi-level sentences.
    3 The focus of the paragraph is the topic sentence.
      4 The remaining sentences are organized in one of two ways.
        5 Parallel repetition is used for emphasis and support.
        5 Chain linking is chiefly helpful for sequencing events and developing ideas.
          6 Frequently, however, we found that the two patterns were both used in the paragraph.

Naturally, studying this chapter cannot guarantee that you will become a great writer overnight. The richness of written language lies beyond analysis and cataloging. But working with the structure of language can give you the tools to communicate with an audience. It can show you how to let others in on your thoughts easily, how to make them remember clearly, how to move and persuade them effectively. If this book has encouraged you to become more aware of the variety of human expression and the subtlety of language structures, it will have helped you on your way to discovering your personal writing voice.

ACKNOWLEDGMENTS

Maxwell Aley Associates: For "Who Flang That Ball?" by W. K. Miksch, from *The Ways of Language,* edited by P. Flug. Crown Publishers, Inc.: For "Snowshoe Thompson and the Wolves" by Dan DeQuille, from *A Treasury of Western Folklore,* edited by B. A. Botkin; copyright 1951 by B. A. Botkin. The Dial Press: For material from *Word Play* by Maxwell Nurnberg; copyright © 1971 by Maxwell Nurnberg. Doubleday & Company, Inc.: For material from *The Travels of Jaimie McPheeters* by Robert Lewis Taylor; copyright © 1958 by Robert Lewis Taylor. Faber and Faber Ltd.: For "Ballad" by W. H. Auden from *Collected Shorter Poems, 1927-1957.* Fleet Press Corporation: For material from *Why Did They Name It...?* by Hannah Campbell; copyright 1964 by Fleet Press Corporation. Harcourt Brace Jovanovich, Inc. and MacGibbon & Kee Ltd.: For "Spring is like a perhaps hand" by e.e. cummings; from *Complete Poems, 1913-1962;* copyright © 1925 by e.e. cummings. Harper & Row, Publishers, Inc.: For material from *Zlateh the Goat and Other Stories* by Isaac Bashevis Singer; copyright © 1966 by Isaac Bashevis Singer. Ann Landers, Publishers-Hall Syndicate, and the Toronto Star: For material from an Ann Landers column. Harold Matson Company, Inc.: For material from *Dandelion Wine* by Ray Bradbury; copyright 1949 by Ray Bradbury. The Province: For "Bad grammar in ads directed at children." Random House, Inc.: For material from *Rabbit Boss* by Thomas Sanchez; copyright 1972 by Alfred A. Knopf, Inc. Henry Regnery Company Publishers: For material from *I May Be Wrong, But I Doubt It* by Mike Royko; © 1968 by Mike Royko. Scott Meredith Literary Agency, Inc. and Arthur C. Clarke: For material from "The Sentinel" by Arthur C. Clarke. The Toronto Star: For "Positive thinking can work wonders for middle-aged" by Gary Lautens. Suzanne Zwarun: For "Lost Language Cause" by Suzanne Zwarun.

ILLUSTRATION

Cover: Paul Klee, *Picture Album,* 1937; The Phillips Collection, Washington, D.C.

Jay Spencer; copyright © 1973 by NAMANCO Productions, Inc., 12. George Silk, 22. Robert Riger, 22. Barton Silverman; copyright © 1973 by NAMANCO Productions, Inc., 22. Canadian Broadcasting Corporation, 37, 38 (bottom right). Miller Services, 38 (left and top). Tibor Kovalik, 47, 54. Magnum: Donald McCullin, 51 (bottom); Elliot Erwitt, 52 (top). NASA, 51 (top). UPI, 52 (bottom). IBM, 67, 68. Time-Life, 110. Canadian Press, 130-131. Fiat, Canada Ltd., 149. Adolf Dehn, 156. Andy Warhol, 165. Barbara Morgan, 174. Walter Chandoha, 176.

Cartoons: Tibor Kovalik, 2, 4, 9, 15, 17, 24, 30, 36, 39, 40, 41, 67, 75, 125, 144. Jon McKee, 25, 104, 105, 112, 141. Macmillan Publishing Company, Inc.: "dogs talking" from *Communications* by Don Fabun; copyright © 1968 by Kaiser Aluminum and Chemical Corporation, 28. Johnny Hart, Field Enterprises, Inc., and Publishers-Hall Syndicate, 15. National Newspaper Syndicate, 42. The New Yorker: drawing by Robert Day; copyright © 1973 by The New Yorker, 100. © 1967 by United Features Syndicate, Inc., 126. © 1973 by United Features Syndicate, Inc., 182.

2 3 4 5 6 7 8 9 76 75